The Edutainer

Connecting the Art and Science of Teaching

Brad Johnson and Tammy Maxson McElroy

Michelle,
Thanks for an awesome
meeting and lunch!
I love your passion for
learning!
Brad

ROWMAN & LITTLEFIELD EDUCATION
A division of
ROWMAN & LITTLEFIELD PUBLISHERS, INC.
Lanham • New York • Toronto • Plymouth, UK

This book was placed by the Educational Design Services LLC literary agency.

Published by Rowman & Littlefield Education
A division of Rowman & Littlefield Publishers, Inc.
A wholly owned subsidary of The Rowman & Littlefield Publishing Group, Inc.
4501 Forbes Boulevard, Suite 200, Lanham, Maryland 20706
http://www.rowmaneducation.com

Estover Road, Plymouth PL6 7PY, United Kingdom

British Library Cataloguing in Publication Information Available

Library of Congress Cataloging-in-Publication Data
Johnson, Brad, 1969–
  The edutainer : connecting the art and science of teaching / Brad Johnson and Tammy Maxson McElroy.
    p. cm.
  ISBN 978-1-60709-612-2 (cloth : alk. paper) — ISBN 978-1-60709-613-9 (pbk. : alk. paper) — ISBN 978-1-60709-592-7 (electronic)
  1. Effective teaching. 2. Communication in education. I. McElroy, Tammy Maxson, 1963– II. Title.
  LB1025.3.J58 2010
  371.102—dc22   2009048756

⊗ ™ The paper used in this publication meets the minimum requirements of American National Standard for Information Sciences—Permanence of Paper for Printed Library Materials, ANSI/NISO Z39.48-1992.

Printed in the United States of America.

Brad: I would like to thank my mother, Carolyn, for her encouragement and support. I would also like to thank my immediate family, especially my nephews Jeremy, Zach, and Josh for reminding me to enjoy life fully and to keep everything in balance. I love you all.

Tammy: I would like to thank my husband, Brian, for always believing in me. To my son Colin, for always striving to do and be your best. To Connor, for always being so supportive and enthusiastic. I love you all.

Contents

Edutainer Program

Acknowledgments

First, we would like to thank Jeff Lyle Johnson for his educational illustrations and cartoons. His ability to portray educational anecdotes in an entertaining manner is reflective of the Edutainer spirit. His countless hours spent in developing these artistic creations are greatly appreciated.

We would like to thank the faculty of the North Georgia University Educational Leadership Program as well as the faculty of the Georgia Southern University Curriculum Doctoral Program. Their scholarly influence has been immeasurable.

We would like to thank Education Design Services for their help in getting this book published.

We would also like to thank the individuals who took the time to share their personal experiences and expertise with us. These include Lily Eskelsen (vice president of the National Education Association), Kathy Cox (Georgia state superintendent), Sylvia Habel (president, William Glasser Institute—Australia), Mary Dimino (comedian, 2008 Gracie Allen Award winner), Chip Saltsman (vice president and North American ASE lead, Capgemini), and Zach Young (head of Wesleyan School). We would also like to thank Joe Richardson for writing the foreword for our book.

Finally, we would like to thank all Edutainers, who make learning come alive for their students every day.

Foreword

Dr. Joe Richardson

This volume is the work of two veteran teachers who understand the lives of contemporary classroom practitioners. The authors rely upon current literature, their own experiences, and the arguments and positions of other seasoned professionals. The uniqueness of their approach, however, is the manner in which they frame their story of creative, imaginative teaching. The issue as to whether teaching is an art or a science becomes an important part of the book.

Utilizing live theater as a metaphor, they argue that teaching, like acting, embraces elements of both science and art: the stage is to the actor as the classroom is to the teacher. That is, just as successful actors are able to transport audiences beyond the stage, successful teachers transport students beyond the boundaries of the classroom. The authors' view is that the science of teaching entails the application of craft knowledge such as planning and delivering instruction, assessing progress, and other organizational and management tasks, whereas the art of teaching is reflected in the teacher's ability not only to transport students but also to connect, inspire, and transform them.

As with theater audiences, classrooms are diverse in their composition, and each has a different set of needs that must be considered in order to connect and sustain interest. The authors of this volume make it clear that the very best teachers are able to integrate these two forms—the aspects of craft knowledge and the art of teaching—and in the process are thus able to create the very best learning environment. This body of work aims to raise the classroom to another level, thereby elevating and expanding the role of the teacher from being a manager to becoming a successful professional who connects with students in ways that bring richness and inspiration to the act of teaching

Great emphasis is placed upon students assuming responsibility for their own learning. Brad Johnson and Tammy Maxson McElroy provide appropriate detailed guidelines as to how this can be achieved. They also remind the reader of the importance of understanding today's students, and also appreciating the fact that contemporary students are accustomed to life in a world where information is readily accessible through many sources. They make it clear that attempting to engage today's students without full knowledge of the technological and electronic modes of communication will not be successful.

The book is presented in a uniquely personal way, neither patronizing nor talking down to the reader. The authors provide appropriate detailed guidelines about how best to approach many of the required tasks associated with creating a successful environment in the classroom. They provide valuable models and strategies for addressing the required tasks of preparing and planning instructional activities as well as how to run, for example, a meaningful go-to-school night program, or how to conduct successful parent/teacher conferences.

While the twenty-first century appears to promise even greater advances in the fields of science, technology, and communication, thus raising expectations for new and exciting educational innovations, there is also every reason to expect that our educators will be facing a whole host of new and difficult challenges. The authors point out, for example, that while access to information will no doubt continue to grow, our ability to educate students to comprehend and utilize this increase in information still remains to be demonstrated. We have yet to prove our ability to provide the educational experiences that result in students being better equipped to interpret, analyze, apply, and adapt the increased flow of information to the tasks at hand.

Yet another challenge confronting our schools is the frequent inability to deal effectively with the increased diversity of our student populations. Teachers are currently experiencing classrooms where many different languages are spoken, languages that reflect cultural values that may differ greatly from their own. The real challenge our schools face is whether or not they will be able to approach this situation without viewing it as an impediment to providing a good educational experience, but rather as a potential for creating a new educational environment that is much richer; such an approach would offer us the opportunity to embrace, respect, and celebrate this diversity, and in the process learn more about the world we live in and how we might go about making it a better world.

Teachers are being asked to narrow their focus and concentrate on improving standardized test results and at the same time they are being asked do a more effective job of addressing the challenges of a changing world; the results of this tension are played out daily in virtually all classrooms across the country. School board policies reflect a more deterministic approach, one that translates into a more controlled approach to schooling. Johnson and McElroy have created a volume that is balanced, comprehensive, practitioner-based, and optimistic in its outlook. They offer hope, inspiration, and concrete proposals about how to make the classroom come alive while remaining responsive to the demands for rigor and accountability.

Likening the classroom to the stage moves us to another level, away from the boundaries that suggest limits and narrow perspectives, to a different sort of arena where we see new possibilities, where imagination and creative impulses flourish and are encouraged. If ever there was a time for an approach such as this, now is that time. *The Edutainer* would be a good resource book across all grade levels and should find its way into teacher training programs as well as staff development initiatives.

Joe A. Richardson, PhD, professor emeritus, Georgia State University; director emeritus, Center for the Advancement and Study of International Education.

(Dr. Richardson served as a public school mathematics and science teacher; university professor; college dean of graduate programs; president of an independent school; and consultant to schools, universities, the U.S. Department of Education, and foundations throughout the United States and abroad. He served on the founding committee of Harvard Principal Center and founded the Principal Center at Georgia State University. He was also a visiting professor/visiting academic at Oxford University, the University of Exeter, and Harvard University.)

Anyone who tries to make a distinction between education and entertainment doesn't know the first thing about either.

—Marshall McLuhan (cultural theorist)

Introduction

Good teaching is one-fourth preparation and three-fourths pure theatre.

—Gail Godwin

The teacher is the most important factor for success of students within the school setting. Yes, it is true. Some may contend that it is standardized testing, reform, accountability, or other initiatives that have been used in the past twenty years. But at the end of the day none of that matters if the teacher in the classroom is not an effective educator. Research suggests that students are most successful when they "feel" connected to the teacher and classmates.

However, teachers who are successful are so because they possess the core skills needed to be an effective teacher. These skills of an effective educator involve communication, organization, planning, management, and developing authentic relationships with students, parents, and colleagues. Just as these "core" skills are important, so is the ability to deliver relevant and engaging information to students.

When the "experts" look to "fix" education, it is often to expand professional training or implement new initiatives that involve more content, curriculum, or the hard skills of education rather than the soft skills. We can all recount the latest bandwagon or many bandwagons that were supposed to be the magic bullet to "fix" education. Whether it is a new teaching model, or more professional development for educators.

Educators in the twenty-first century must take a different approach to teaching if we are to prepare students for an ever-changing world. The

Edutainer rationale is the paradigm shift that is needed by teachers to be highly effective educators. An Edutainer is a combination educator and entertainer. This individual possesses such traits as vulnerability, wit, excitement, humor, and, most important, a desire to motivate students to excel.

When you think about an effective entertainer and an effective educator there are striking similarities. It is these similarities or principles that will be presented in this book. Think of someone like Jerry Seinfeld, Jeff Foxworthy, or Bill Cosby, who are considered effective entertainers. Among the many entertainers in the industry, these individuals stand out because they have been successful, but what are their keys to success?

First, they are visionaries. They understand that a change in culture requires a change in methods and presentation. They make their material relevant to present culture. They also have self-confidence or would end up with stage fright and not be able to perform.

Preparation is also vital to these performers. They organize and plan their material long before they get on stage or they would bomb the performance. But they also have to be effective communicators or the material wouldn't matter anyway. Finally, they have to deliver a performance that is relatable to the audience or they would be booed off the stage.

Now think of the highly effective educator. She is also a visionary who understands that students want relevant and relatable experiences in the classroom. The effective educator has to organize and plan her lessons before she teaches them. She has to manage her time and scheduling to get all the content areas covered. She needs effective communication skills and self-confidence to deliver the information effectively.

Finally, she also has to deliver the information in an applicable and relatable manner, or the students will be disengaged. So, as you can see, there are many similarities between an entertainer and an educator. When these skills are utilized effectively, the Edutainer will deliver a stellar performance.

The story behind the Edutainer concept is based upon the collaborative effort of the authors' more than thirty years of combined teaching experience at the K–12 and collegiate level within public and independent school systems. Through these experiences, advanced degrees, and scholarly research we discovered and quantified what made us different and developed the key principles for success in the classroom of the twenty-first century. While we both knew intuitively we were unique in our approach, we also knew our approach delivered extraordinary results year after year.

When we met eight years ago, we realized that we shared these same characteristics and principles of effective teaching. We enjoyed teaching, were entertaining in our delivery, had high expectations of our students, and made real world application to the material. We also understood the importance of involving everyone in the educational process and developing authentic relationships with students, parents, and colleagues. Therefore, the Edutainer concept presents methodologies for teachers to thrive, enjoy, and feel empowered while producing a learning environment where students are engaged, responsible, and successful in "owning" their own learning.

And now you know the rest of the story.

—Paul Harvey

ACT I

THE VISION

SCENE 1

Connecting Education with the Twenty-First Century

Many of our schools are good schools if only this were 1965.

—Louise Stoll and Dean Fink

As a visionary, the Edutainer understands that culture plays an important role in shaping our lives. Education often views the influences of culture as irrelevant to learning, when in reality it is an essential aspect of the learning. Movies, music, television, video games, and other media outlets have a profound influence on learning. In fact, research suggests that media and pop culture may be the most important means through which children are educated. Therefore the effective educator embraces cultural changes as an opportunity to connect learning to the real world.

Embracing these cultural influences not only makes learning more engaging, but also makes it more relevant as well. With the technological explosion of the "Information Age," students have access to unlimited information at their fingertips. The Internet, a cell phone with Internet access, laptop computers—the list goes on. If our culture has changed so dramatically, why has education remained relatively unchanged? Especially when culture plays such an important role in the shaping of our children's education?

Even business has been influenced by cultural change as we transition from production type goods to service oriented industries in a global economy. Education in the twenty-first century must make a transition from the traditional education of assembly-line mentality, rote memorization, and antiquated thinking, to education that utilizes the cultural resources available to make education relevant to students and to the present-day world in which we live.

As the name "The Edutainer" suggests, there are many similarities between an educator and an entertainer, but there is one conspicuous difference. The entertainer makes her ideas, dialogue, or performance relevant to today's culture, so the audience finds it relatable. If a stand-up comedian used references from fifty years ago most of the audience would not be able to relate, and there would be the proverbial "cricket sound" to break the silence.

Well, guess what—education is still presented much as it was fifty years ago, and yet we expect students to embrace it passionately. Would they embrace a black and white television with only three channels or a video game that only offered the game *Pong*? How excited would your child be if you told him you were going to buy a new stereo, but that it only had an eight-track tape player?

Think about the fact that even organized religion, which is often steeped in old tradition, has adapted to meet the needs of children in our current culture better than schools. Even from a business perspective, how effective will a student be when he enters the business world if the extent of his education is to sit still, take notes, and memorize information for a test?

We will examine the relevance of education as it relates to a changing culture. We will then look at the relationship between teacher, students, and parents. Finally, we will provide strategies to build and improve authentic relationships within the school community.

Cultural Influence

The world of the twenty-first century is very different than the world of even twenty years ago. Everything from technology, media, entertainment, and the business world have all gone through a major metamorphosis. However, one striking antithesis to this trend has been education, which has remained relatively unchanged. One glance into a classroom would find very little has changed over the past twenty or thirty years. If education has not kept up with the changing times, then one has to question its relevance in preparing students for the world of tomorrow. As we connect education with the twenty-first century, it is important to first examine the influence that culture has on our world today.

Business Influence

If one of the goals of education is to prepare students to be productive citizens who are capable of entering the workforce, then there appears to be a major disconnect between business expectations today and the educational process. For example, between 1995 and 2005 the U.S. economy lost three million production jobs, while creating seventeen million service-related jobs. This reinforces the belief that students need to develop their interpersonal and relational skills to become a productive member of the workforce.

Another aspect of the changing economy and job market is the interaction we have with other countries. It is important for our students to be prepared for a world that is smaller than it has ever been. There are about one billion people in Mexico, China, India, and other countries that have risen from poverty to the middle class over the past ten years. This means about one billion potential clients, business partners, consumers, or even competitors for products and services around the globe.

These people, just like U.S. consumers, now spend more money on leisure activities and entertainment at a higher rate than ever before. In fact, much as in the United States, these people now see as necessities many items that were revered as luxuries just a short time ago. This new middle class is also competition for jobs in a global market. These people are on taking jobs abroad that were once monopolized by people in the United States.

For instance, a lot of jobs for organizations have been outsourced to other countries, such as India, because their job force is increasingly capable of performing in these job markets. The jobs of today and especially tomorrow, do not require memorizing information to perform repetitive tasks; technology and automation have made these tasks obsolete. But the core and interpersonal skills required in today's global market will only become even more essential tomorrow.

In this information age, management, relational, and communication skills are vital to success in the real world. Therefore, the Edutainer focuses upon developing the relational and interpersonal skills of her students. She also exposes her students to other cultures so they can better appreciate the customs and practices of diverse cultures. This opportunity can only enhance the student's preparedness for the twenty-first century.

Media Influence

Culture has changed more dramatically in the past two or three decades than at any other point in history. Would you believe that a cell phone has more technology than even government agencies had just thirty or forty years ago? Consider all the other changes that have occurred in our culture over the past thirty years. There are hundreds of television channels to watch compared to only three or four channels thirty years ago. There are channels for home shopping, golf, weather, cooking, and even an outdoor channel, so you don't actually need to go outdoors anymore. Unfortunately, with all the channels that are available, television has lost some of its value.

Think of the great advice that was given by Andy Griffith, or the parents on *Leave It to Beaver*. How many television shows and teen movies can you think of today where the parents are seen as wise and instrumental in the development of their children? Rather today, television and movies portray parents as slow-witted, aloof, and easily manipulated by their children. The children on programs today are seen as more intelligent than their parents. We have come a long way from the wisdom of *Father Knows Best* to the most famous line of the bumbling Homer Simpson, "Doh," which unfortunately has become a part of our cultural language.

It appears as though the media is slowly "dumbing down" America. You have to look no further than the present reality shows to see how television has sunk to an all-time low. And how does someone like Paris Hilton become an icon simply because she was born to a rich hotel owner? Will the next national icon be the child of William Becker, the founder of the Motel 6 chain? Even when surveyed, guess what most children want to be when they are older? A lawyer or doctor, you say? No, they want to be famous. When children would rather emulate Miley Cyrus, Tom Brady, or Julia Roberts than do well in school, it does pose a challenge for education in the twenty-first century.

Fortunately, the Edutainer is up to the task and understands the importance of making education applicable to the lives of the students. She understands that part of this responsibility is to make the students educated consumers. Because of the influence of media, corporations, and businesses, students need to become aware of the power of these entities to persuade and manipulate their decisions and possibly even their beliefs. The Edutainer utilizes authentic relationships and relevant teaching to connect education with the real world.

DID YOU KNOW . . . By the time the average child reaches the end of his high school years, he will have spent more hours watching television than attending school. Talk about a culture change!

This doesn't mean that the students don't assume the responsibility for their own success. Actually, the students have a very active role in the process and ultimately take ownership of their learning when an effective learning environment is created.

A Different World

To see how education might be connected with the twenty-first century, we will examine how culture has changed in the past twenty or thirty years. We must also examine how the individuals associated with education (students, parents, teachers, and administration) are influenced by these cultural changes. It is, after all, a different world today.

Educators: Yesterday and Today

One major difference between the antiquated teacher and the Edutainer is the involvement of everyone in the educational community. The antiquated teacher doesn't seek interaction with parents, but prefers working in an isolated environment. This is often because she is not equipped to handle confrontation, or possibly lacks the confidence to engage in genuine conversation with parents or others.

However, the Edutainer embraces interaction with parents because it is beneficial for the student and her. She welcomes dialogue and building authentic relationships with all the cast members in the performance. She sees this as an opportunity to develop classroom support for the students and herself.

What is an authentic relationship you may ask? It is a relationship built upon respect between all the members of the school community. Each member has responsibilities in developing and nurturing these relationships. All the cast members are important because of the experiences and abilities they bring to the educational community. It takes the whole "village" or educational community to produce a stellar performance. So, let's examine the cast members and the cultural influences that affect relationships in the twenty-first century.

Students' Attitudinal Differences

The demands on the youth of today are much more intense than even ten or twenty years ago. There is much more pressure to get into college, to make an athletic team, and to be accepted by peers in a culture that emphasizes outward beauty and being popular as the major focal point of youth life. Because of this pressure many students appear more interested in social life or athletics than in formal education. Keeping up with the trends is of key importance to students. Unfortunately, our culture only perpetuates this emphasis on outward beauty through the advertisements, television shows, and movies.

Because of the societal demands and attention placed on youth, many children feel a sense of entitlement. It is this sense of entitlement that makes it hard for students to see beyond their immediate wants and focus on education. As Chip Saltman (vice president of Cap Gemini) explains, "There is an attitudinal difference in children today versus two decades ago. Children lack a stick-to-it-ive-ness."

He continues, "When I was a hiring manager, I preferred not to hire people from Stanford or Harvard because they felt like they were entitled to a job and should be running the company. The best hires were actually people that went to night school and worked during the day. These people often had a better work ethic. These people stayed with you for many years and were a benefit to the company." Students today often seek to "be" understood rather than seeking to understand others. As you can see, students' attitudes, motivation, and values are shaped by our culture.

Me, Me!

This isn't the name of the secretary on the *Drew Carey Show*, but rather the focus of our students' lives. Our culture teaches students to seek only what is pleasurable and brings immediate gratification. For instance, when a child is watching a program that he or she is not interested in, the child can simply change the channel and locate a more satisfying program. Another problem with television is that an issue is posed and solved in the neatly packaged thirty-minute segment. Therefore students are conditioned to think that problems should be solved quickly and easily.

The entertainment and sports industries have perpetuated the "me" mentality that affects our students. They portray life as one big party and suggest that you are only acceptable if you are beautiful, dressed well, and maintain a lavish lifestyle. But think of how much focus is placed on children, especially boys, to excel in sports. They are given the best equipment, the best trainers, and a personal chauffer (usually Mom) to drive them around to their practices and sports, so they do begin to contract that dreaded "it's all about me" syndrome.

Not that there is anything wrong with wanting the best for your children, but when they are treated as the center of the universe, then guess how they begin to act? You guessed it—like the center of the universe. Okay, so can you begin to see now how our culture influences us, and even hinders education by glorifying an almost anti-intellectual culture that pursues becoming a star of music, movie, or sports rather than valuing the need for education to attain your ultimate goals?

Recreational Isolation

Another area in which children today differ from yesterday's children is that they are much more isolated. In the past, children were free to roam the neighborhood and play with other children. Today, parents are more guarded about where and with whom their children play. Children often come home and lock themselves in until their parents come home. They spend this time watching television, surfing the Internet, or playing video games, often alone. Students are also drawn to an isolated form of communication and relationship that is typical of electronics—phones and texting, video games, and Internet surfing. Have you ever noticed how kids that are together spend time texting people that are not there rather than speaking to the ones in their presence?

Remember the comedian Sinbad? He often talked about the changes that have occurred in our culture. In one particular instance, he talked about how everyone in the neighborhood would take care of each other, but they also knew your business. When a child got into trouble everyone in the neighborhood would know about it. Sinbad recalled one time when he got into trouble, and the neighbors knew about it before he got home. He said he didn't just get a whipping when he got home, but he got a whipping by the neighbors on his way home. Sinbad said that reflecting back, this attention from the neighbors made him think twice before he did something wrong in the future.

Unfortunately, many children today don't even know most of their neighbors. The point here is that there is much less social acclimation at a time when students need to be developing their interpersonal skills.

Students today are also technologically savvy from an early age. It seems that children can masterfully operate a video game before they even learn to walk. Think of the amount of time spent watching television, playing on the computer, and playing video games. Children spend approximately thirty-eight hours per week watching television, surfing the Internet, and playing video games. So, how can a child sit and play a video game for hours at a time but have trouble sitting still in a classroom for forty-five minutes? Maybe it is because they feel education is not connected to their life.

It is important to examine the influences on students' lives and incorporate them into the learning process rather than dismissing them as distracting or lacking importance to education. This is not to say that all cultural

When asked if the word was spelled correctly, Edmund replied, "I dont know, where is the spell check button?"

Figure 1.1.

changes are bad. When students are so technologically savvy, for instance, then there are opportunities for them to show their creativity in presentations. For example, if the technology were readily available, why would a teacher now require a student to give a presentation with a poster board as a visual aid rather than a PowerPoint presentation?

The Edutainer embraces changes in culture and learns to relate to students through their interests whenever possible. There was one student at our school who loved video games. He would go home and spend hours playing video games everyday. He wasn't that interested in school and didn't participate in after-school activities, nor did he feel a connectedness with his peers or the school. However, we decided to have a video game night at the school where the boys in his grade level could spend the night and play video games.

He showed up early for this event. He was a very good "video gamer," and as the night went on, everyone wanted to be on his team, which won every game. Many of the students started talking with him and he enjoyed the attention. He was in the spotlight for once and he felt good about himself. Talk about a change in the demeanor of a student.

The next Monday he seemed like a completely different student. In class he was more engaged and now had a common experience with other students to talk about. Imagine, something as simple as a video game night that can change the attitude of a child about school and education. The importance of this story is not that the student was entertained, but that a connection was made between his school and him.

Authentic Relationships with Students

The authentic relationship with the student is particularly important because the teacher has the potential to greatly influence the student. Don't continue to perpetuate the antiquated "taskmaster" style of teaching. This style is where you fill the students with information and expect them to sit still and memorize information. The authentic relationship allows the student to become an active rather than a passive participant.

Whether it is your rules, expectations, or how you deliver your material, keep these thoughts in mind: Am I presenting the material in a manner that is engaging for the students? Am I treating them they way I would want someone to treat my child? At the end of the day remember they are still children, facing real problems in a tough world, so they need all the support they can get. And you as an Edutainer can be an important part of the equation.

As we leave this section, here are a few ideas that you will want to remember as you build authentic relationships with your students.

- *Responsibility*. Give students responsibilities, so they feel vested in the class and educational process. Students, especially younger ones, enjoy having specific tasks that they are assigned during the course of the day. Many of these duties are discussed in the organization section. Students also take responsibility in the ownership of their learning. As relevant learning is introduced, students will become more active in their own educational process.
- *Know their world*. This has been done in part for you as we have examined the culture in which students now live. Become familiar with the student's interests, leisure pursuits, and activities, so that you better

understand them. Remember, building relationships is the key when learning is personalized.

- *Establish common ground.* Discuss things of common interest (news, community happenings, and sports). Look for special interests the students have, for example, the names of favorite TV shows, leisure activities, video games, music, and so forth. Take their interests and incorporate then into the lessons for relevancy at least as an introduction or for examples or analogies that can be shared.

- *Sense of community.* Be approachable to the students. Make sure they are comfortable with coming to you with problems, issues, and support. This means you are willing to exhibit a level of vulnerability, to "be real" with the students. Remember children can detect when adults are sincere and truthful. They can also detect the disingenuous adults as well and will keep a wall between themselves and those adults. Help students think of the class as "we" rather than in terms of "I," "you," or "they."

Understanding Parents

Many adults today have one of the toughest and most demanding jobs—being a parent. The job of parenting is not made any easier by the generational gap that exists between parents and their technological savvy children. This generation gap exists because parents grew up with limited technology, while their children appear to be cyborgs (part human and part computer). Lily Eskelsen (vice president of the NEA) explains that when it comes to technology, "Kids are fearless natives and their parents and teachers are more like immigrants who don't speak the language." While the Edutainer is technologically savvy, she is aware that parents may not be, so she communicates in methods other than the computer, such as students' agendas and weekly folders.

The dynamics of the home life have changed in recent years as well. In most cases, students today live in a single-parent home or a home where both parents work. In fact, since the 1970s the number of working moms has almost doubled from around 30 percent to nearly 60 percent. Research also shows that Americans work approximately 160 hours more per year, or the equivalent of an extra month per year, than they did twenty years ago.

Perhaps "Keeping Up with the Joneses" has become our new national anthem. However, parents often feel a sense of guilt for the long hours at work and time spent away from their children. Because of this guilt, there is a small percentage of parents who try to buy their children's affection or become their friend rather than be their parent. These parents often purchase

DID YOU KNOW . . . Parents spend only 3.5 minutes per week in meaningful conversation with their children.

their children presents in place of parental gifts such as support, guidance, and limitations.

These are also the parents who will act more like a lawyer than a parent when their child exhibits poor behavior or weak study habits. They don't want to discuss the issue; they only want the teacher to "fix" the problem. They are looking for a quick answer, rather than an opportunity for their child to learn from the experience. It is easier to be their child's friend than it is to be an authority figure.

During our years of teaching, there was one instance where a student was in trouble, and the parents were called in for a meeting. They were very upset and felt like the teachers were treating their child unfairly. Within a few minutes, the student was actually arguing and talking back to his parents. The parents became more frustrated, so we asked the student to leave the room.

The parents immediately expressed their own irritation with their child. They went on to explain that their reaction to us was really in response to their frustration with the child, versus the situation at school. The mom broke down in tears and began to explain that they didn't know what to do with him. The parents had taken away the child's phone, computer use, video games, and yet he continued to misbehave.

Having dealt with literally hundreds of students over the years, we offered some suggestions to help us all work together in getting the student back on track. One thing we mentioned was that when a child has everything taken away, he may feel a sense of hopelessness. Therefore, he has no desire to change his behavior. We brought the student back in the room and together as parents and teachers set up a contract between the child and his parents. For example, if he didn't get in trouble for "x" number of days, then he would earn something back like his phone. If he continued to do well, he would gain back other privileges.

There are two lessons that are relevant from that actual experience. First, if a parent lashes out at you, understand that the frustration may have nothing to do with you or the classroom situation. Secondly, when there is open and honest dialogue between parent and teacher, real solutions materialize to best support the student.

It is important for the educator to learn to relate with the parents of the twenty-first century. First, remember the parents have a story, and they have a vested interest in the education of their child. So, respect their role and work to build a relationship that allows ownership in the educational process.

Authentic Relationships with Parents

Now let's examine the following ideas which will help you build strong relationships with parents.

- *Respect.* The Edutainer understands that in order to receive respect, she must give it first. Therefore, all respect begins with her.
- *Responsibility.* Encourage the parents to assign responsibility to their child. This is actually more difficult than assuming the role themselves. Teach the child to do for himself versus having the task done for him.
- *Failure is not the end.* Parents want the best for their child and some have a hard time allowing their child to be unsuccessful. Make the case for growing independence by explaining how important it is that their child learn to be responsible. This may mean having the room to fail. Students will make mistakes. Part of maturing is learning how to recover from these mistakes.

Some of the most important learning experiences and life lessons have come through struggles. A parent is doing a disservice to their child if they don't allow them the opportunity for these experiences. How will the student be able to function when he enters the work world? Will the parent still be bailing them out? Encourage parents to have their child learn from his mistakes.

Teachers: Partners in Crime

Teaching can be one of the most isolating and stressful professions. Much of a teacher's work is in an isolated classroom that detaches her from the support of her colleagues. No wonder the attrition rate among new teachers is almost 50 percent by their fifth year of teaching. One of the most important aspects of collegiality is the sense of community that it builds among teachers. Research even suggests that collegiality among teachers has a positive correlation with student success.

The Edutainer understands that in the twenty-first century, education can no longer be an isolated profession. We have already discussed the importance of developing relationships with parents, but it is time for the effective educator to reintroduce herself to her "partners in crime," her colleagues. Effective teachers are a great resource of knowledge, ideas, and even activities that can be shared with teammates. Collaborating may seem like a

DID YOU KNOW . . . Teachers spend only about forty minutes per day conversing with colleagues, and the topics mainly involve materials and discipline.

foreign idea in a profession that is known for its isolative qualities, but today's culture requires a new relationship among all the members of the school. It is important to have a relationship with your peers that are both supportive and positive.

Here are a few strategies that will help you forge better relationships with the partners at school.

- *Be collegial.* In essence this means to build and nurture relationships with the faculty and staff. Create a respectful environment through positive interactions with your peers. Discuss more than just discipline with your colleagues; get to know your staff personally as well.
- *Be professional.* Remember you are a highly qualified educator, so exhibit professional traits. Keep conversations positive, supportive, and confidential. The image you project will determine the way you are treated by others.
- *Value the expertise of colleagues:* Share ideas, thematic units, and innovative assignments with each other. Someone may already have an idea you have been looking for. No need to reinvent the wheel.
- *Be a mentor.* You are a great resource for a novice teacher. Mentoring is also beneficial because it allows you to reflect on your own skills and methods as you help your mentee. Be a leader in the school and support those in need.
- *Sense of community.* Remember teaching is often perceived as an isolated endeavor. However, the faculty is really a team that needs to work together. A school environment has a profound affect on the overall functioning of that school. If teachers are vested team players and work together, then students will greatly benefit.

Partnering with the Principal

The job of principal has become more demanding through accountability, educational reform, and other factors. This is especially so in public school administration, where a principal's job is measured by standardized test scores rather than the overall effectiveness of the teaching and learning environment. When you think of the pressures and time spent in an administrative role, it is easy to see why principals may feel the "burnout" that a teacher may feel.

Remember, administrators have to deal with the parents, students, and faculty within the school as well. So, how does the Edutainer maximize her relationship with administration? How do you perform "outside the box" when your administrators typically want you tucked away neatly in the box with your standardized tests, antiquated text book, and the latest reform initiative? This is hardly a recipe for a stellar performance.

The purpose of this section is to give you strategies in building a collegial relationship with your administration. Remember, the Edutainer is a highly qualified educational leader, so exhibit professionalism in the relationship. Don't forget that this individual is ultimately responsible for your continued performances, so make the effort to include this person in the show as much as possible. Here is a list of strategies that will help you build a professional relationship with your administration.

- *Occasionally share good news or ask your principal's advice.* Avoid only visiting your principal when you have problems. Invest time in nurturing a positive relationship. Only through frequent interactions does mutual trust evolve.
- *When your principal has done something helpful, drop him or her a note.* Let the principal know his or her efforts are appreciated. Everyone needs a pat on the back every now and then.
- *Take the initiative to invite your principal to visit your classroom.* You are the Edutainer, after all, and your lessons will be innovative and cutting-edge. So, when you are giving an encore perfomance, try to schedule an observation. Strive to view the principal as an instructional ally.
- *Choose your battles carefully.* In any relationship you only have a limited amount of credit available in the other's emotional bank account. Don't squander your assets on minor gripes; save it for the truly important issues. However, we have always found there will come a time when you actually do have to choose to engage in a battle. If it's that important, engage the issue head on.
- *When you take a problem to your principal, prepare a couple of possible solutions.* Be concise in your presentation. Be practical in what you expect the principal to do to solve your problems.
- *Try to help the principal get his or her job done effectively.* Submit grades, attendance records, and reports on time. Your professionalism is an asset to everyone involved.

Edutainer: Performer

What separates the Edutainer from the traditional teacher is an awareness of cultural changes and the ability to adapt and flourish in a changing culture. So let's reflect on the essential characteristics that make the Edutainer so effective.

Characteristics of the Edutainer:

- Exhibits the three Rs: respect, relationships, and responsibility
- Master of her content, competent
- Well prepared, organized
- Relevant teaching; applicable to real world; practical
- Enthusiastic; passionate about teaching
- Approachable, friendly, available.
- Concerned for students' success
- Has a sense of humor, amusing
- Warm, kind, transparent
- Has a command of and interacts well with her audience
- Provide a "warm classroom climate"
- Works hard, plays hard—makes this philosophy contagious to her audience

Edutainers care about their students, learning, and the educational process. They also make it relevant and as much fun as possible. The success of the Edutainer lies in her confidence and competence to make learning as applicable to the real world as possible. Remember, the Edutainer doesn't just think outside the box; she threw the box away. The Edutainer performs "on stage . . . in the spotlight . . . with an engaged audience." Before we leave this section, we would like to leave you with a few of our "Oscar-winning" tips that will leave your audience shouting "Encore!!"

Oscar-Winning Tips for the Edutainer

- *Make the connection.* Connect the material with the real world. Make learning relevant and applicable to the students' lives. A constantly changing culture requires education to be flexible and continually seek relevance.
- *Be personal.* Have your personalized stories handy. Think about some things that have happened in your life that you have learned from or that would be applicable to specific classroom topics. This is being

vulnerable and open to the students. They sense when you are genuine. Plus, it is an Edutainer's best tool to grab and hold someone's attention.

- *Be likable.* Smile—a lot. Encourage—a lot.
- *Be believable.* You want to establish trust and your credibility with the students.
- *Listen . . . listen . . . listen.* Communication is a two-way street. Listening may be the most important trait of communication. Listen, learn, and grow.
- *Close the loop.* Whatever personal information you gather from your students, circle back around and see how things are going.
- *Guest stars.* The community is full of experts and other entertainers, so incorporate them into the lessons. See examples given in the "Intermission Performances."
- *Enthusiasm is key.* Having a hard day and not feeling like teaching? Get into a habit of picking a stop before you enter the classroom or stepping "ON STAGE." At that point, all the baggage is tossed away and you are ON. Lights, camera, action! Put yourselves into a state of enthusiasm . . . excitement . . . fun! Excitement is contagious!

SCENE 2

Director's Chair

Leadership is about responsibility and action, not title or position.

—The Edutainer

The Edutainer understands that the traditional role of the teacher has to change to be effective in the twenty-first century. The teacher is no longer the instructor that works in isolation, but has to be a leader in the educational community for learning to be effective. It is our conjecture that the teacher is the most influential aspect of student success in education.

However, the teacher often lacks a complete range of skills that build her self-confidence to fully maximize her potential. For example, when Georgia's State School Superintendent Kathy Cox was asked about challenges facing new teachers, she said, "Many teachers underestimate their abilities and expertise." Therefore, if teachers were to exhibit confidence and competence in their abilities, they would be more effective leaders as well as effective educators.

Much like an entertainer, who not only performs but also gives input into the directing and production of a performance, the effective teacher must assume responsibilities beyond simply teaching a class of students. The amount of responsibility and leadership you are given may be dependent upon your administration or school dynamics.

For example, there are some schools, which classify themselves as democratic schools, where teachers have more input into policy making, such as curriculum and discipline as well as other functions of the school. This would

DID YOU KNOW . . . The fear of public speaking is considered the number one phobia in the United States.

be the ideal setting for a teacher leader. But if the teachers do not possess the proper skills to lead, even a democratic school environment will not realize its full potential.

Our strategies for leadership are not for you to simply serve on a committee or give input into new textbooks. If these become the only aspects of responsibility, then your impact on the educational community is limited. As an empowered leader, you will possess the skills to influence the whole learning environment, so students will have the opportunity to be more successful. Thus, the goal of this chapter is to provide strategies for developing leadership characteristics that will empower you to become an Edutainer in the twenty-first century.

Overcoming Stage Fright

One of the first steps in developing leadership qualities is to be comfortable with public speaking. In fact, speaking in public is considered the top phobia in the United States. The fear of public speaking is also commonly referred to as "stage fright." Jerry Seinfeld's take on public speaking is that "the average person at a funeral would rather be in the casket than doing the eulogy."

If public speaking is one of the top phobias in the United States, then it is safe to assume that there are educators who have this fear as well. If you have ever felt dizzy, high levels of anxiety, butterflies in the stomach, or even broken out in hives (yes, we have actually seen individuals break out in hives) before speaking, then you may have a fear of public speaking. However, since teachers spend a lot of time in front of audiences (classroom, workshops, parent meetings, open houses, etc.) it is important to alleviate this fear so you appear to be a competent and confident professional.

First, it is comforting to know that your audience will most often be a group of children rather than adults who may scrutinize you unmercifully. This is not to say that the students won't analyze you to some degree, but hopefully there is a lower stress level when the audience is a group of ten-year-old children rather than a room full of Fortune 500 executives. So before we examine the Edutainer leadership traits, here are a few quick tips to remember as you step on stage.

- *Have confidence.* Remember, you are the expert in your content areas as well as pedagogy.
- *Preparation.* Have lesson rehearsed. Include talking points, handouts, or even a PowerPoint presentation.
- *Repetition.* The more you present, the more comfortable you will become.
- *Be early.* Start every day relaxed and focused. Have handouts copied, or information organized before starting the day. Have a few minutes of quiet time before the students enter the classroom.
- *Be calm.* Take deep breaths and smile—a lot!

Leadership Characteristics of the Edutainer

An effective teacher is also a teacher leader. While some traits may be inborn, many traits can be improved upon when attention is given to them. The characteristics listed below are part of the skill set that makes the Edutainer so effective. But in essence every section of this book will give you confidence and competence to become an effective leader. However, our focus in this section will particularly be focused on the traits and strategies needed to be a "lead" performer in the twenty-first century.

There are a lot of characteristics that are attributed to an effective leader. For the purpose of empowering the teacher; we have established the seven leadership characteristics of the Edutainer. While no list ever compiled on any topic is all-inclusive, we feel these are the foundational principles for becoming an effective educational leader in the twenty-first century.

- Be competent.
- Lead by example.
- Exhibit passion.
- Assume responsibility for your role in the process.
- Develop a sense of responsibility in students, peers, and parents.
- Be a risk taker.
- Demonstrate flexibility.

Often lists of leadership characteristics are just that, a list. However, to really develop and utilize these characteristics there needs to be an explanation of their concepts. Therefore this chapter is devoted to examining these seven characteristics in detail, so that you can understand and develop these characteristics as you grow into a leader. These characteristics will benefit you in the classroom, the school setting, and the educational community beyond the school walls.

Wouldn't it be refreshing if teachers felt empowered enough to step outside the school setting and influence the educational process in a larger arena? Shouldn't the actual teachers in the "trenches" be giving the most input into school reform and policies, rather than a politician or a theorist with no real practical experience?

The leadership characteristics will be examined and strategies offered to maximize each trait. This will equip the educator to make better decisions and draw upon these strategies when the need arises. With these strategies, you should become confident enough to step outside of your comfort zone and seek to be an agent of change for education in the twenty-first century.

Be Competent

Competence is the ability to perform specific tasks effectively. Competence as it relates to teacher leadership can include subject content, methodologies, and even decision-making skills. When a teacher demonstrates a high degree of competence in her teaching abilities, she also exhibits a confidence that is tangible to her audience. This doesn't necessarily mean that you need a PhD to feel competent in teaching mathematics, but it does mean that you need to prepare and understand the material before covering it. The following are a few strategies that will help you feel competent when you step into the spotlight for a lesson or presentation.

Have a Plan

Strategies for planning will be discussed in detail in a later section; however, as a leader, it is vital to have goals, objectives, and plans. If you have no idea where you are going, how do you know when you get there, or if it's even where you want to be? Therefore, to be a successful leader, it is important to have goals and objectives. These goals and objectives also need to be clear, detailed, and defined. To define your goals you have to first ask yourself questions.

- What strategies will you utilize to make learning relevant to the students?
- What kind of influence would you like to have in the educational setting beyond the classroom?
- How will you include the community in the educational process?

These are some of the questions that you will need to examine as you prepare for your school year.

DID YOU KNOW . . . 75 percent of executives claim that good physical fitness is crucial to achieve career success at executive levels.

Fit to Lead

While teaching is considered one the most rewarding careers, it can also be one of the most demanding. With very few breaks, and only a twenty-minute lunch it is easy to find yourself heading to the vending machine or reaching in your desk for chocolate to satisfy your hunger or worse to help yourself de-stress. Improving your health is an important aspect of being an effective leader. A healthy body is a confident body. This doesn't mean that you need to be a supermodel or a bodybuilder. But it does mean that you need to take care of your body and health by eating healthy foods, managing stress, and making healthy decisions at school and at home.

For example:

- Set goals for including leisure activities into your daily schedule.
- Understand that not everything will get done each day.
- Drink water during the day.
- Keep healthy snacks in the room.
- Avoid vending machines and keep no candy in your desk.

Lifelong Learner

This terminology has been used so often that it may have lost some of its importance. However, competence increases as your knowledge, skills, and abilities increase. This is actually one area where teachers excel more than other occupations because most teachers typically enjoy learning. Lifelong learners don't expect their degree and a few years experience in the classroom to be sufficient in keeping up with a changing culture. Maintaining a passion for learning will allow you to keep up with latest research, methodologies, and technology, which will in turn make you a more competent educator.

- Stay up with technology.
- Observe other teachers—especially if they share the same content area or grade level.
- Join professional organizations.

- Attend workshops within your content areas or subjects of interest that you can incorporate into the classroom.

Before we leave this section it is important to note that one of the most important traits of a leader that exudes competence is the use of communication skills. Communicating your goals and objectives may be one of the most important aspects of any leadership role. However, rather than discussing this important topic in a few sentences, we have devoted an entire chapter to communication.

Lead by Example

Leading by example means that you are a role model. You don't just set expectations for students; instead, you are the epitome of modeling them. In this capacity, you are hardworking and always portray yourself as a professional. Leading by example means that you would never ask someone to do anything you aren't willing to do yourself. Remember, as an Edutainer, you want to create the optimal learning community for your students. Be an example to the rest of the community, so they will embrace and pursue your vision as well.

Visionary

How many times have you seen someone do something and you say to yourself, "I could have done that"? As a visionary, you are looking at the best way to perform in the classroom. You don't even mind if you fail, if it ultimately helps you become a better teacher. This may mean learning how not to do something. As a visionary you are not intimidated by problems or responsibilities but rather you embrace them because they give you the opportunity to shine in the spotlight.

The Edutainer, for example, understands that culture has changed, which means the people within the culture have changed as well. This doesn't mean business as usual, but rather it means you have to understand the influence of those changes. You can then make education more effective, relevant, and applicable for the educational community.

Examples of this would include:

- Be vulnerable with your students. They know when adults are genuine and when they aren't. They need to know you are in their corner and want them to succeed. For example, disclose a weakness you share with a heroic figure in a novel.

- Find creative ways to use technology. Make videos with the students.
- Let students teach the class. Public speaking is a skill they need to develop as well.
- Revisit novels that are used in class. Maybe you could switch one of the classics for a contemporary work that is more relatable to today's culture.
- Make learning real-life rather than disconnected. For instance, in math, create a store for the students to learn certain skills, rather than simply rote memorization.

Proactive

One the most important attributes of a leader is to be proactive rather than reactive. Reactive means that you spend most of your time "playing catch up" or "putting out fires." Preparation is an important quality of being proactive. If you are prepared for the day, then when an issue arises you are better prepared to handle it.

Being proactive means to anticipate issues before they arise, so you have a plan in place. This means that rather than reacting to issues, you actually create the actions that happen in the classroom and during the school day. For example, if you have a "bell ringer" or word problem on the board each day, the students know to come in and get to work rather than talking and goofing off.

Other ideas for being proactive in the classroom include:

- Have solid (Edutainer) lesson plans each day. Plan from bell to bell.
- Set a specific time each day to respond to e-mails.
- Be consistent with consequences to rules.
- Schedule time for handling paperwork, for example, grading papers, inputting grades.
- Have all materials ready for each day.

Embrace Confrontation

This means that you are assertive and confident. You don't mind confrontation, which poor leaders shy away from, because you are up to the challenge. Confidence is essential to becoming a successful teacher. In fact, your school life and classroom will be a very different environment once you exhibit a confident persona to students, colleagues, parents, and administrators. This doesn't mean that you are a bully or that you don't know how to compromise. But there comes a time when you actually have to pick your battles.

Having the confidence to speak up is important because when issues are expressed openly, it leaves little room for rumors and gossip. This is one of those areas that may be difficult for some people, like public speaking, so here are some strategies to help you face any conflicts with confidence.

- Don't personalize situations; keep conversation to the facts that are involved.
- Communicate concerns to parents early.
- Keep excellent records. It's hard to dispute written documents.
- When meeting with parents about issues, greet them warmly, allow them to vent, and make sure to share something positive about their child.
- Relax, breathe deeply, and focus on issues, not emotions.
- Listen, listen, and listen. Many times, a person is frustrated and simply needs to vent. Their issue with you may actually be misplaced anger about something totally different.
- Focus on positive outcomes.
- Always follow up a serious meeting with an e-mail. Then detail the issue, resolution, and goals moving forward.

R.E.S.P.E.C.T.

This is one aspect of leadership that is important to model to the students. If you want your students to be respectful to you, make sure you are respectful to them as well. Remember that every member of the cast has an important role and the performance can't run smoothly unless everyone is working together.

Another important aspect of respect involves your role in the classroom. Some teachers worry so much about whether the students like them that the students often don't respect them. These are the teachers that often try to pacify students, so they will behave in class. This environment is not built on respect and is not a healthy place for the teacher-student relationship to subsist. Here are some strategies for exhibiting and showing respect in the educational community.

- Follow through on consequences; keep your word.
- Don't gossip.
- Remember the Golden Rule!
- Be consistent. Have high expectations for behavior and keep them.
- Don't be afraid of confrontation.

Exhibit Passion

As an educational leader you need to be passionate about your role and the people around you. Some teachers get into education because they are passionate about a subject; others have a passion for working with children, while others have a passion to give back to the community. Regardless of the specific reason for becoming a teacher, passion is essential to becoming an Edutainer. Your passion will also be one of the most influential aspects of your relationship with your students. In our research, participants revealed that passion was one of the most important traits of teachers that influenced them in school.

Mary Dimino (comedian) recalled, "I remember in high school I had a favorite English teacher. He wouldn't just sit behind a desk and teach out of a book or with his back toward us writing on a black board. He stood up and used the classroom like a stage. He owned it. All eyes were on him. He conveyed passion for what he was saying along with the theatrics needed to keep an adolescent's attention." So, as an Edutainer, make your passion contagious to everyone in the educational community.

Care

There are curriculum theorists who believe caring is one of the key components to education. In a sense, this is true because if you don't genuinely love and care for children, then you will never maximize your potential as an educator or educational leader. In fact, I think it is safe to say that if you don't love children, regardless of a love for math, science, and so forth, then you probably need to consider another profession.

Children need to feel a sense of security, safety, and care if they are to be successful in the classroom. It is our belief that students perform better when they feel a sense of connectedness with their teacher and the classroom. Remember the old saying: "Students don't care how much you know, until they know how much you care." If you have a passion for students, then you will exhibit a genuine care for them.

- Ask students about their weekends or activities they are involved with.
- Inquire about a student's "off behavior." Ask if they are having a bad day.
- Show care to every student not just the ones who demand your attention.

Humor

A sense of humor is part of the art of leadership, of getting along with people, of getting things done.

—Dwight D. Eisenhower

The Edutainer needs to have a sense of humor. Humor is a way to relate and connect with all the different members in the cast. Humor also allows you to create a comfortable and more relaxed atmosphere. As with any entertainer, it is also important for the educator not to take herself too seriously, but this doesn't mean that you aren't professional. Laughing at yourself is a sign you have self-confidence and this allows the students to see you are in fact human.

- Share a joke or a funny story with the class. Relate it to subject when possible.
- Remember, humor keeps students' attention.
- Be careful of sarcastic joking. This doesn't mean sarcasm can never be used, but you should know your students well and have a strong rapport with them.

Connection

When students feel connected to their teachers and classmates, their achievement levels increase. This connectedness is what makes the teacher such an integral component of the student's success. Just as the entertainer has to make a connection with the audience, an educator must as well. In fact, the comedian Brian Regan has said that one of the most important aspects of his stand-up is to establish a connection with the audience as quickly as possible. The Edutainer understands the importance of connecting with her students to keep their interest. She also makes a concerted effort to connect with parents, colleagues, and administrators as well.

- Learn students names and interests as soon as possible (see name game in intermission).
- Use positive reinforcement. Everyone loves a "pat on the back."
- Connect beyond the classroom. Make the effort to observe students outside of school, such as their sporting activities, performing arts, or other interests. This offers a great opportunity to connect with their parents as well.
- Contact parents to share good news about students. They like to hear their child is doing well.
- Share stories. Some of the best entertainers are the ones who make a connection through personal stories to which the audience can relate. This is true of educators as well.

Inspiration

As an effective educator, it is important for you to make the students feel like they have value and abilities. Sylvia Habel, president of the Glasser

Institute in Australia, explained it this way: "My favorite teachers inspired me by articulating their belief in me . . . their enthusiasm for their work and their positive attitude towards their students was inspirational." When students feel like you believe in them, they often work harder and become more successful.

How many times in your own life have you worked harder when someone complimented you, or commented positively on your ability? Exhibiting your own passion about learning can also motivate students. Many of you can probably recall a teacher who had a passion for a subject like science or language arts, which actually made the subject enjoyable and relevant to you. What are the keys to inspiring others?

- Remember why you are a teacher. The love of students, subjects, and helping others.
- Use praise and positive reinforcement.
- Present information in unique and enthusiastic ways.
- Make each student feel special and important.

Assume Responsibility for Your Role in the Process
As an Edutainer you actually serve multiple roles in the educational process. You are an educator, entertainer, colleague, employee, mentor, advocate, and expert.

The Edutainer is not intimated by the responsibility of these roles but rather embraces the opportunity to shine in the spotlight. The success of the Edutainer is not simply in understanding each role, but having the ability to transition fluidly between the roles. In one instance you might need to be an encourager for a student, but in another instance you need to be the authority figure that gives them a sense of safety. As the producer, director, and performer, it is your responsibility to make sure the stage and cast are prepared for an optimal performance.

Be the Thermostat
Much as a thermostat determines the climate of a room, the effective educator is responsible for the climate of her classroom. It is the educator that creates the type of learning environment that will exist. Your attitude can make it a great day or a gloomy day. You have influence on whether learning is enjoyable or torturous. As the leader, you alone are responsible for the climate that exists in the classroom.

Therefore, it is important for you to make the most of that responsibility. Make learning enjoyable, relevant, and applicable. Make your classroom a place that students enjoy rather than a place they dread. Furthermore, it is important to set the climate for the school community. If you "set the climate" then you are positive and proactive when it comes to your job, students, parents, and the administration. Here are some useful strategies in setting the climate for your class:

- Create a safe and engaging learning environment.
- Focus on solutions, not the problem.
- Make everyone feel important and necessary.
- Start every day fresh with a positive attitude.

Reflective

We all have heard Socrates' saying, "The unexamined life is not worth living." Examining or reflecting upon your actions is not always an easy task, especially when you spend your days with a room full of children. Our research suggests that children today are not reflective, meaning that they are inundated with information, yet don't take the time to reflect on what they know, learn, or experience. In a sense they are smarter, but not wiser. The same can be said of adults and especially teachers, who wake up and hit the floor going full speed. There is little time to stop and analyze what we have done.

However, there needs to be a time of reflection and self-analysis, so you can analyze work, relationships, and most importantly your decisions. It is through thoughtful reflection that you can assess and make changes to improve your teaching performance. Reflection is significant in every area of your life and its value to an educator is no less important. Here are a few questions to reflect upon during the school week:

- Are my daily lessons effective?
- When do I make time to reflect?
- What can I do differently? (lessons, meetings)
- What roles am I not fulfilling? (mentor, colleague, leader, encourager)
- Are my goals and expectations realistic?

Emotional Stability

This is the ability to handle stress and thrive under pressure. This can also be described as mental toughness. An emotionally balanced educator is an effective educator. Students need a safe and stable environment in which to learn. If, as their leader, you have trouble dealing with issues, then the students will react accordingly. Emotional stability means to address issues objectively rather than subjectively. When it comes to issues you are passionate about it is sometimes easy to be frustrated, angry, or even scared. However, as the educator and leader, you have to maintain your composure and keep your emotions under control regardless of the situation.

Here are a few tips to help you "keep your cool" and even alleviate some of the stressors that could cause problems:

- Don't overreact to an issue, or personalize it. If you become emotional, walk away and take a deep breath. When you are calm, readdress the issue objectively.
- Expect the unexpected. Plan, plan, plan.
- Organize. Being organized can help you handle the unexpected.
- Leave work at work. Home is your retreat from the classroom. When you enter the school, leave everything else at the door.
- Take time for "you." Start a new hobby. Find an activity that you enjoy and stick with it.

Develop a Sense of Responsibility in Students, Peers, and Parents

This is one of the most important roles for the director aspect of your duties. The education process is more effective when all stakeholders take responsibly for their part in the process. In our culture, there appears to be an expectation that the teacher is responsible for every aspect of the learning. While the teacher has an integral role in the process, she can't do everything. So, one of the leadership qualities of the Edutainer is to develop a sense of responsibility for the other members of the cast. If they have roles and responsibilities in the process then they will feel more connected and vested to the learning process.

Empower Others

The best leaders understand that it is important to empower others. While you may feel like you have very little power to share, in reality you have many responsibilities that could be delegated to others. Students who are given responsibilities or chores in the classroom will immediately feel more vested in the classroom. Many students, especially younger elementary students, take the chores very seriously and are very territorial about their duties. If you are or become a department head, include team teachers in responsibilities that you feel they can handle and that will boost their own self-confidence.

Edmund teaches the "language of texting".

Figure 2.1.

Even parents can be given responsibilities such as planning field trips or holiday parties. As an effective leader you should take your director role seriously. When everyone takes on roles and responsibilities, it prevents you from feeling like you have to do it all. This will be beneficial to your long-term health and sanity. As you delegate responsibilities, here are some important strategies to remember:

- Give responsibilities that you feel someone can manage successfully.
- Give praise often and publicly.
- Encourage open communication.
- Ask for input, especially from colleagues.
- Ask to be someone's mentor.

Everyone has a Role

As cultural changes influence education, the roles in education also change. This means that the dynamics of the people involved also change. In the past, it was assumed that the teacher did it all. Even today, there are parents who think it is the sole responsibility of the teacher to make sure their child is educated. However, in our present culture, with the media, technology, and all the distractions vying for the students' attention, it is important for everyone to become more involved in the educational process.

As an Edutainer it is your role to encourage participation from everyone. The performance, or team effort, is not effective unless everyone is involved. If the Edutainer has cultivated authentic relationships as discussed in the first chapter, then getting involvement from others is not difficult. When determining roles for others keep these ideas in mind:

- Define roles and responsibilities of others. Define limits of authority and expected outcomes.
- Include everyone in the process (students, parents, colleagues, community).
- Be an effective communicator. Make sure everyone is on same page. Communicate expectations frequently.
- Encourage and inspire continually. Find someone in the act of doing something right and offer praise.

Be a Risk Taker

Are you a risk taker? Have you ever tried something unique or unusual? Risk taking doesn't mean that you throw caution to the wind and try things that may be dangerous. But it does mean stepping outside of your comfort zone. Risk taking is actually your willingness to try new things based upon your strengths, abilities, and even weaknesses.

Sometimes this means stepping outside the box and trying new or innovative ideas to make learning relevant in a changing culture. Risk taking in the educational setting can be as simple as speaking up in a meeting or something more difficult like offering to teach a workshop. In this section we examine some of the characteristics of risk taking that are relevant to the Edutainer.

Vulnerability

Vulnerability is a trait of entertainers and educators alike. Think of the comedian that gets on stage and shares her personal experiences with the audience. This can be a frightening experience, but it makes her act believable and relatable. If you want students to find you believable and relatable then you must be vulnerable as well. This is an important aspect of building relationships and leadership.

While vulnerability may sound simple, it is not always easy to be open and transparent with others. While self-disclosure of your weaknesses to others may seem frightening, it can actually improve and strengthen your relationships. As you prepare for the year keep these tips in mind:

- Share stories with students. Personal stories are a way to relate to students and show your humanity.
- Laugh at yourself. Humor is disarming and it shows you don't take yourself too seriously.
- Be willing to try new ideas.
- Don't be afraid of failure. As a coach once told his athletes, there is only winning and learning—not winning and losing.
- Never be afraid to ask others (colleagues) for help.

Teaching Outside the Box

This doesn't mean you need to teach every lesson standing upside down on top of your desk while juggling with your feet. But it does mean you have to do more than teach straight from the textbook. The Edutainer teaches outside the box by making learning relevant in a changing and diverse culture. Make learning relevant to their needs, not simply memorization from outdated material.

For instance, in our changing culture, students need interpersonal skills to be successful. Remember, as an effective teacher, your goal is to "reach" the students. To think outside the box requires someone who is confident, competent, and capable of thinking differently with an open mind. How does outside the box thinking translate into the classroom?

- Let students do more group projects, or presentations to work on those public-speaking skills.
- Change the stage for the performance. For example, rather than teaching science in the classroom, take them outside to experience the world in action.
- Focus on the value of finding new ideas and acting on them.
- Encourage, respect, and nurture others when they come up with unique ideas.

Fear of Failure

A fear of failure is one of the greatest obstacles to achievement in an adult's life. It is this fear that keeps us from trying new and innovative things. However, risk takers do not fear failure. It's not that they necessarily enjoy it, but they do not let it control their actions or limit their goals. The occasional failure that accompanies risk not only builds character, but also is an opportunity for reflection and growth. It is a fear of failure that limits many individuals, including teachers, from maximizing their abilities and talents. It is easier and "safer" to do what is familiar. Many almost take pride in the fact that they have done the same thing for ten years or twenty years.

However, the Edutainer wants to push the boundaries, and maximize her potential. If she tries something new, it doesn't matter if she is successful or not—she has taken action. If you are willing to take the risks, then the rewards can be great. Here are some ideas to consider:

- Revise your definition of failure. Think of attempting nothing as actual failure.
- Consider the missed opportunities of not trying something new.
- Failure, with proper reflection, can actually be a positive experience.

Demonstrate Flexibility

One of the most important traits of an effective leader is flexibility. Flexibility means to adapt behavior and work methods in response to new information, changing conditions, or unexpected obstacles. This is especially important when you are an educator. It is easy to spot an educator that is not flexible. She would rather work in isolation, balks at ideas for change, and likes her "routine" because she is familiar with it.

However, the focus of education is student success, not teacher appeasement. If our culture is in a state of constant changes, then, as educators, we need to be flexible and fluid, so we can adapt to those changes. For instance, if the students behave, does it really matter whether they sit in their desks, or lie on the floor to take notes?

Willingness to Change

In a culture of constant change it is impossible to be an effective leader if you cannot adapt to changes. How many times have you heard a teacher say something like "Well, I have fifteen years of teaching experience, so I know what works." They haven't adapted or grown to the point that they have a variety of experiences, but feel that "time served" is sufficient to make them an expert. An individual that rests her laurels on simply "years of experience" may limit herself to opportunities of growth. A willingness to change shows that you have the students' best interests at heart, because you know that the world they will enter is different from the world of yesterday.

- Be accepting of ideas from others.
- Realize you don't know it all.
- Remember student success is the focus, not your complacency.
- Learning and trying new things will keep you young!

Expect the Unexpected

When dealing with children you have to be ready for anything. Even in the classroom, you never know when there may be a fire drill, when a child may vomit on a desk, or even when the oven in the cafeteria will catch on fire complete with news helicopters flying overhead, yes this really happens! Teaching keeps you on your toes. The best way to expect the unexpected is to be proactive and prepared. For instance, you never know when you will become sick, so make sure you have adequate work and plans for a substitute. During the winter, students are more likely to share colds or the flu, so make sure you prepare for the outbreak with tissues, antibacterial hand wash, and so forth.

Be prepared; yet be willing to go with the flow when the need arises. For instance, if a student were to get injured or even lost on a field trip, don't panic and become part of the problem. Everyone is looking to you for stability, so take a deep breath, assess the situation, and then make a thoughtful decision on what to do. Here are some strategies to help alleviate some of the fear of the unexpected:

- Never let them see you sweat. Regardless of what is happening, work quickly to resolve the situation without adding to the problem.
- Always have a backup plan, or plan "B."
- Keep a sense of humor.
- Remember the students look to you for security, so maintain your composure regardless of the situation.

If you develop the seven leadership characteristics of the Edutainer, you will be more confident in the classroom and the school setting. The

Edutainer is not only an expert teacher, but is an asset to the school and the educational community. Remember that you are the expert, and you understand the needs of education in the twenty-first century. If you will embrace the changes of culture, while including everyone in the performance, then you will be able to produce, direct, and ultimately perform in a production that is worthy of Edutainer of the year!

Stress SOS

In our fast-paced culture, everyone is inundated with stress. We wake up to the alarm clock buzzing, which means the day is started by stress. From there the day only gets worse, as we fight traffic in a rush to get to school. We work all day, fight traffic home, and then the rest of our day begins. Every evening we try to recover from the day and prepare to start it all over again the next morning. If there is one word to describe our culture it is *stressful*! The Edutainer understands that stress can not only impact her health, but can also influence her decision-making and leadership skills.

In the mid-1800s, many British merchant ships lost their ships at sea because they were overloading them with cargo. So a member of British parliament, Samuel Plimsoll, introduced legislation to regulate the loading of ships to prevent more ships from sinking. This included a load line mark on the ship, so a ship could be loaded until this line touched the water and then no more cargo could be added. This became known as the plimsoll line and it prevented ships from being overloaded and sinking while at sea. This line is still in use today as a standard measurement to prevent ships from becoming overloaded and making them vulnerable to sinking.

Well, guess what? We all have a plimsoll line, and if we are overloaded with pressure and weight we may sink as well. Our sinking comes in the form of stress, sickness, and burnout. One of the reasons for early teacher burnout is that many responsibilities are placed on new teachers and they aren't equipped to handle them all well. Many of the responsibilities are in addtion to teaching, such as coaching, sponsoring clubs, service on committees, and other duties from which veteran teachers may shy away.

DID YOU KNOW . . . The adverse health issues in 43 percent of adults can be related back to the stress in their lives.

Why is it important to deal with stress? Teachers work in what experts say is the "dirtiest job" in America. That means they are exposed to more germs, bacteria, and viruses than any other profession. So, keeping your immune system strong is important to an Edutainer. This means dealing with stress and taking care of your body.

This also means ensuring that students take precautions to be healthy as well. This can be as simple as keeping hand sanitizer available so students can keep their hands clean. Think about how hard it is to have an engaging class is you are sick or several of your students are sick. This is not an effective learning environment. So, how can you overcome the SOS of stress?

- Start the day with a routine: arrive at school early enough to sit and reflect on the day to come.
- Keep water handy to drink throughout the day. Not sodas or even diet sodas.
- Have an exercise routine. Even if it's taking a walk in your neighborhood in the evening.
- Eat healthy. Bring your lunch if the cafeteria doesn't offer healthy alternatives. Don't be a vending machine marauder.
- Don't forget leisure time. The school day does end. Make sure to spend time with family, friends, and just yourself.
- If you become sick, rest until you are well.
- Wash your hands often, especially during flu season.
- Laugh and enjoy life!

The Edutainer assumes a lot of responsibility in the educational process. She is not only a great performer, but also has a vision for directing education into a new direction for the twenty-first century. It takes confidence and a certain amount of risk to teach outside of the box. But the old saying, "high risk, high reward," could never be truer. Remember that your goal is to provide the optimal learning environment for student success. As we leave this section, remember these Edutainer tips for empowerment.

Empowerment:

- *Believe in yourself.* Don't be critical of yourself or your failures. Thinking negatively about yourself is one of the greatest causes of limitation in life.
- *Love yourself!* Remember, if you don't love yourself, you can't love others.
- *Take control of your health.* It's hard to be empowered if you are unhealthy. A healthy body is a confident body.
- *Discover and use your talents.* Understand that your passions are often your talents. Cultivate them to their fullest potential.
- *Think, plan, prepare.* Be proactive, not reactive. You will be in more control of situations.
- *Balanced life.* Make sure that work doesn't become your whole life. At work, maintain positive relationships with all stakeholders.
- *Enjoy the journey.* After all the planning and hard work, don't forget to relax and laugh at yourself; remember that laughter is cheaper than a hospital visit.

INTERMISSION 1

Guest Stars and Performers

While the Edutainer is vital to the success of the students, it is of great value to incorporate other guest stars into the performances whenever possible. It is also important to include the students, so they feel a sense of connection. Therefore, we have provided some suggestions to create a dynamic and guest-filled cast for a memorable performance.

Guest Stars

As noted in the tips for the Edutainer, your community is filled with individuals with talents and abilities that can be utilized in the educational setting.

This can include local celebrities, business people, artistic individuals, or anyone that has a story or a talent to share with the students. So don't be afraid to contact individuals in your community at large. You may be pleasantly surprised at the people who are willing to make a guest appearance.

Some of the guest stars that we have invited to speak in the past include:

- Eight-time Mr. Olympia Lee Haney spoke about attitude, goal setting, and working to be a better individual. He discussed how he came from humble beginnings but through hard work and perseverance, he became the top bodybuilder of all time, even surpassing Arnold Schwarzenegger's record. The students were enthralled by his size and were mesmerized by his presentation.

- We invited Chris Gardner, a missionary from a school in South America (Peru), to speak about his experiences helping the needy in the Amazon jungle. He is a real "Indiana Jones," who has canoed down the Amazon River, eaten *cuy chactado* (fried guinea pig), and experienced many incredible adventures in his years in South America.
- Dan Cathy (president and COO) of Chick-Fil-A spoke to our students about having a servant's heart. This mission belief reflects the focus of Chick-Fil-A: service. He stressed the importance of helping classmates, family, and those who are less fortunate. Cathy also talked about goal setting and living a balanced life. He shared his experiences of wrestling in college and how he loves to play the trumpet with a band.
- We even invited a local police officer to speak to a health class about drugs and alcohol. He brought the "drunk" goggles, which distort vision, as well as photographs of accidents that were DUI-related. This officer was personal and engaging in his discussion of this dark topic. He left a sobering impression with the students about the potential deadly affects of drug use and DUI.

Groups

There are different organizations that offer educational opportunities for schools. Some of them offer their services free of charge while others charge a nominal fee, so there is flexibility based upon the economic ability of your school or students.

Some of the guest groups that we have utilized in the past include:

- The Georgia State University Bio-Bus, which is a thirty-foot long, self-contained, mobile laboratory that can accommodate up to fifteen students at a time. It travels to public and independent schools around the state. The bus offers a variety of teaching modules, such as the heart, weather, chemistry, and much more. The Bio-Bus is publicly funded to create a free, high-tech program available to all students in the state. The Georgia State University faculty, staff, and students operate the Bio-Bus program.
- High Touch High Tech is another program that provides in-school field trips. This program does charge a nominal fee but offers a variety of modules that are geared toward elementary-age students. These

include activities associated with space, earth, life cycle, fossils, energy, the body, and much more. Their programs are designed to fit the standard objectives of the school curriculum. These are interactive modules, where the students do most of the experimentations, and the scientists simply explain the concepts to help the students experience and enjoy the various science activities.

• Canine Assistant is a nonprofit organization that trains and provides service dogs for children and adults with physical disabilities or other special needs. In addition to physically assisting those with disabilities, Canine Assistant service dogs are instrumental in removing many of the barriers faced by the disabled in today's society. The organization offers a free educational presentation, which educates students about disabilities and the roles that service dogs play in society. In addition to the important health benefits, the dogs provide both physical and emotional support for the recipients.

There are many other organizations in the community that offer presentations or programs that can benefit schools. Some of these include the local police, EMT, or fire departments. There is no reason why an Edutainer can't incorporate the community within the educational process, so the gap between education and the "real world" is bridged.

Student-Focused Performers

If there is one area in which students can become stars themselves, it is in giving back to the community. Many independent schools do a good job of providing service opportunities for students because part of their goal even in a college prep program is to develop the whole person. This idea includes service projects that affect the immediate community and also the world at large. However, in the public schools, while there is an objective to develop a productive citizen, we need to encourage more of the general population of students to learn about citizenship and experience the opportunity in giving back to the community.

Even though county or school policies don't necessarily establish a schoolwide service project, there are many opportunities for the Edutainer to consider for the students to give back to the community. A class service project allows students to develop as citizens while helping those that are less fortunate. It is a great idea to have someone from a charitable organization speak to the students prior to getting them involved with the organization.

The experience can be better understood and become more meaningful when the students are prepared ahead of time.

Here are some of the activities that can be used to get the students involved:

- *Food drive.* Simply collect canned foods for a food bank or local soup kitchen. Allow students who participated in the food collection to have a hat day or extra break. This extra reward also serves as a bit of positive peer pressure because the students are given a fun day and are identified as a person who chose to help. The focus here is not to make the prize extravagant but rather to focus on helping the particular charity. We did this schoolwide, and in one morning we actually filled an entire school bus full of canned foods for the local food bank. This was a rewarding experience for all.
- *Clothes drive.* This is a variation to the food drive but can be done with clothing or simply coats. Set standards for the clothing received, such as it should be new or only slightly worn. The upcoming season dictates what type of clothing is collected, for example, getting ready for a cold winter or sharing summer clothes.
- *Toy drive.* Here again this can be as simple as students bringing in board or video games, game systems, or accessories that they no longer use or are simply willing to give to someone else. These can then be given to local charities during the holidays or to other organizations such as children's hospitals. If needy children are in your school, they could be used for them as well.

Assisted Living Centers or Orphanages

Many organizations within school often have service projects or service hours that are required as part of a membership in a club. However, all students need to experience helping others in the community. This builds a sense of otherness, and students have the opportunity to lend a helping hand. This is especially important with the elderly or with children needing a family. Unfortunately, our culture, unlike other countries, does not promote spending time with the elderly or referring to them for advice.

Instead, our pop culture encourages students to look elsewhere to get this guidance. This is all the more reason to set up a time for students to visit the aging citizens in their community. This can be a very rewarding experience as the students can see that the elderly enjoy the company and have some interesting stories to share. Spending time with children in need will provide joy for these kids and at the same time help the students appreciate their own families and all of the possessions that they have been given. You might even want to have the students make something to personalize the visit and have a gift to leave with them.

Other Organizations

Many colleges and universities are placing more weight on the extracurricular activities that students have done in high school. They are looking for well-rounded individuals that can contribute in a variety of ways to the college experience. This demand places greater importance on the services and projects that students participate in during their high school careers. So, these activities not only create an internal reward for the students, but also help them with entrance to a preferred college. There are many organizations where students can help out with their time and labor.

ACT II

THE REHEARSAL

SCENE 3

Planning

Proper preparation prevents poor performance.

—Charlie Batch (NFL quarterback)

One of the most overwhelming tasks as an educator is setting up the classroom. The organization chapter provides great insight into both the physical as well as the systematic use of all of the classroom equipment. However, the Edutainer begins with a plan before even moving the first desk or hanging the welcome sign. Much like a play or movie production, the setting couldn't be identified without the notion of the first act.

Preparation

We suggest trying to get into your classroom before the actual preplanning week begins. Those of you who are entering the teaching profession for the first time are probably wondering why you would want to begin your year early if the school already allows for almost a week of getting ready for the school year. Doesn't make much sense, does it? Unfortunately, most school systems today allow for very little time spent working in the classroom.

The workday usually revolves around faculty meetings for class placements, yearly updates and expectations of the school's curriculum standards, scheduling, and assignments of extracurricular duties. Time is also given for companies that provide insurance and investments in the savings plans. Needless to say, the week is long over, and the classroom teacher ends up

Dorothy asked for a week of pre-planning, without meetings, so she could actually plan.

Figure 3.1.

spending most of her weekend prior to the first day wishing she had known what she knew now about allotted time in the room. Enter the planning stage.

Preparing the Stage and Scenes
Prepare a "Before Act I Checklist." This is a "to do" or a "to create" list of all of the tasks that have to be done before the first day begins. These simple suggestions allow the Edutainer to stay focused and methodically determine what needs to be bought, made, and set up or done. Most importantly, it eliminates the incredible amount of stress that the beginning of every school year brings in the overwhelming feelings of not knowing where to start and the "oh yeah, I need to remember to do this" moments that strike in the middle of the night.

We strongly recommend filing this list to be used the following year. More than likely many of these tasks will be duplicated but also tweaked as you become more experienced or perhaps pick up different subjects or classes along the way. Being able to pull up this list eliminates having to start from "square one" every year. Remember, the Edutainer learns to think not just for one scene but over the long term, as in the entire production. Accomplish a task the first time, but do so thoroughly.

The "Before Act I" Checklist

- Arrange desk placement. Refer to the organization chapter to discuss the different styles of structuring the room. Teaching style and age of students requires thought before randomly creating desk patterns. Traffic flow and mobility between desks also need to be considered.
- Make a label for each student desk. This is especially important during the first few weeks of school as it provides a routine of where every student is to sit and affords you the opportunity to memorize names.
- Create a seating chart for the substitute folder. Refer to substitute folder section in this chapter.
- Gather materials for learning centers (games, drawing books, crayons, etc.). Remember, these are activities that can be used as transitional opportunities when students finish at varied times and also for rewards.
- Set up supply table.
- Organize supplies that students will be using in bins/plastic drawers. Label each (pencils, erasers, red pens for editing, expo markers, tape, staples, staplers, rulers, colored pencils, crayons, markers, glue, rubber cement, scissors).
- Separate paper. Especially construction paper to accommodate holiday and special units, lined and graph paper, drawing or copy paper.
- Create/label bins for turning work in to be graded—for example, subjects or classes.
- Label cubbies or hooks. Students will use these to store gym shoes, books, book bags, or jackets. Remember to coordinate student names with numbers.
- Gather books for classroom library, color-code each for different genres, and make a small poster to explain the code (e.g., "red dot" fiction, etc.).
- Gather and label resource materials—for example, thesaurus, dictionary, atlas sets, jump drives, and discs.
- Make schedule for the week, including Monday–Friday. Hang using pockets sold at teacher supply centers. Use colored index cards—one color for each day of the week.

- Create classroom jobs wheel, using creative theme ideas.
- Create student name cards to show who is being assigned to do what job for the week.
- Create and post a list of posters to hang on the wall for information. What will you need to make these and what will each communicate? For example, one might include "What to Do During Homeroom" or another might show "Proper Heading," "Class Rules," and "Class Expectations." These are all the visuals that will express daily routines. Don't forget "Emergency Procedures" too, such as fire or tornado drills. Walls in the classroom should look attractive but should also either serve an informational purpose or share students' work.
- Plan/purchase bulletin board items for hallway or classroom. Think about how the boards might be used to either introduce new topics of lessons or display individual work. Preview chapters that will be covered throughout the year.
- Determine what kinds of charts your classroom will need—for example, birthday, growth, reading, math facts, or other measured skills.
- Compile a list of items that need to be purchased so that you can make one if not two trips when getting your classroom ready.
- Create a substitute folder. Refer to full substitute section discussed later in this chapter.
- Select a planning and grade book. Before randomly buying the cheapest book or possibly using the free one given by the school, give this book some thought. Does it allow enough room for all of the lessons and transitional times that you experience on a daily basis? Is there adequate room given for each lesson to be written with any type of details?
- Pre-write all holidays and special events. Do so in the actual lesson plan book so you'll remember these when writing the lesson plans three months later.
- Set up grading book with student names, subjects, and grading periods. Yes, we realize that most assessments, whether using actual numbers or even narratives, are done using a computer program. However, having a backup if for some reason the grades are lost or in question is a wonderful resource for a person responsible for holding the red pen. Refer to management for more details.
- Organize any monthly projects, such as reports both written and oral; determine dates for these, too. We'll discuss this in more detail with the actual planning process.

- Organize and label all teaching curriculum such as teacher editions of workbooks, texts, and extra practice editions. Label each under subject headings as "Reading" or "Math," including your name. It seems a bit silly to think you have to label a reading resource "Reading" but so many books cross-reference different subjects and lessons with more emphasis on one area than the other. By the time you get around to using the book, you might not remember what you had thought about using it for your actual lesson or activity.
- Find a place in your classroom to house all of these items together. If you teach a variety of subjects, finding the book in your lesson plan and being able to smoothly transition it into your activities can be a challenge when you have twenty-some students looking and waiting for you to collect your thoughts as well as your book.
- Set up the teacher desk and organize supplies. This would include items such as grading pens, stickers, folders, and stationary items. Are you a big list maker or do you jot down ideas on the small pads of paper that stick to another page? Be prepared going into the year and know you have what you need.
- Set up filing systems: one for general, subjects, and students' work.
- Organize daily forms such as attendance, lunch, monies collected—create a folder for each in the general filing section of your room.
- Organize folders such as "To Grade," "To Copy," or "To File." These are especially important when using an assistant as this avoids wait time if you are teaching and your aid isn't sure where to locate or how to handle items.
- Create Agenda board.
- Have any First Day information written on board that would be helpful in expressing the daily lessons or directions. This is especially important for the first few days as you are waiting for the students to all arrive and establishing a morning routine. Overcommunicate your expectations and directions for individual work to emphasize acceptable standards.
- Review student records and or files. The Edutainer does believe in meeting her students without any preconceived notions from other teachers. Starting fresh is an opportunity that all students deserve each fall. However, there will be certain situations and needs that you, the teacher, would benefit from knowing without causing any embarrassment to the student or family or which might help you better serve this individual during the learning process.

- Check with counselor or administrator for any special needs child preparations. Again, while doing homework in setting the stage for the upcoming production, the Edutainer realizes that there is a wealth of knowledge in her fellow stagehands. The counselor as well as an administrator serves different needs than the classroom teacher. Use them as a support system, which will only further benefit all of your intentions in creating an optimal learning environment for each upcoming student. If these individuals have had past experience with your new student(s), they can save everyone some time in beginning where the school left off last June instead of starting from scratch.
- Remember too that guidance counselors fulfill a different role to the student's family, too. The counseling department provides a safe haven for sharing pertinent family life knowledge that the regular classroom teacher might not be made aware of in the beginning of the year. By working together, all of the players involved benefit and are afforded an optimal opportunity to succeed.
- Review all major chapter topics for set curriculum. This helps when knowing what to plan as well as purchasing appropriate themes while shopping for classroom items.
- Set meeting times with fellow teachers and record set faculty meetings in personal calendar. We find that the more information is in one place, the easier it is to keep up with classroom, faculty, and nonadministrative duties. This could include carpool and extra club assignments. Use the professional agenda idea if not your own planning book.
- Create lesson plans for the first week of school.
- Copy and gather any materials that are needed for first week of lessons.
- Get a treasure box or bead store ready along with a brief description of prices or points to obtain items.
- Write friendly letter to introduce yourself to parents and students. Be friendly, and welcome your students to the new year, and be professional by explaining your expectations or goals you plan to accomplish together.

Drop-Ins
Many schools particularly in the lower elementary classes, or even private schools for that matter, allow for a designated time for parents to drop by with their children and meet their teacher. This can be done in a casual open house style or beginning the school year with a quarter or half day. This time presents an opportunity to put a face with a name, become familiar

with the location of the classroom, and possibly an opportunity to drop off required student supplies. Being that each parent and student will have several questions and that you will need to keep the crowd moving, presenting the following information on your board will help you meet each family in a time-friendly fashion.

For Your Information

- Lunchtime
- Recess time
- Are snacks allowed? If so, what are some suggestions?
- Contact information for you—list email address, school phone number
- Contact information for them—list columns on a sheet of paper that call for the student's name, parents' names, parents living with student, parents' e-mail addresses, parents' home and cell numbers (see handout in the appendix, pages 164–65)
- Consider having a conference sheet that is ready for sign-ups including dates and times
- Sign-ups for volunteer positions or simply a willingness to help for coordinating future opportunities such as a "room parent"
- Carpool/bus information for the first week of school
- Compile forms that need to be completed and returned during first week of school
- Reminders or forms for nurse questions or medications that will be stored in the clinic
- Supplies—be prepared for parents to bring in supplies, and have a place in mind for where you would like them to put these items

In the past we have used colorful clip art that we copied, printed, and cut, such as a phone, bus, or big yellow pencil. We then had a typed form for each and taped it under the visual to the front board. Next, we numbered each idea so that parents could see there were maybe seven points that you wanted to share or collect information from them. This colorful and informative approach allowed us to say a brief hello to both parent and student and welcome each to the new year. However, we weren't bogged down with repeating each item for every new person who walked into the room. Using our front boards, we were free to welcome our new families and also presented a professional and organized view of ourselves.

The Opening Act

There is nothing more exciting and nerve-racking than the morning of the first day of school. Regardless of whether this is your first day of teaching or you are a veteran returning to your own classroom, expectations are high, and everyone is feeling a bit anxious. "Jitters" are completely normal for both the teacher and student. The unknown seems to bring out the fear or at the very least some anxiety in all of us. The Edutainer realizes this and therefore plans accordingly.

So, exactly how are you to get the entire cast functioning seamlessly throughout the day without anyone's missing his cue and needing help with his role? Practice, practice, practice. And this will take more than one day of explaining and rehearsing.

Let's begin with the introduction. First impressions are priceless, and there are no second chances. Your success for the remainder of the year will be determined by the first few weeks of school. The Edutainer wants her students to feel comfortable and know that she is competent not only in her content knowledge but also with knowledge of running the show. Students will feel comfortable when they know that they are in good hands and where everything is kept in the classroom. Remember, the goal for the first few weeks of school is to build a community within the classroom, establish student accountability, and teach methodologies for achieving that responsibility. The following are some guidelines for establishing a successful first day of the school year.

First Day: Scene 1, Take 1, Action!

- Be at the door or in the front of the room. Greet them: look each student in the eye as they enter the room; smile—let them know you are happy to be here!
- Provide both verbal and written directions as to where to sit and put belongings, and have something for them to do while waiting for others to arrive. This could possibly be having them fill out some information for you to keep or assembling their supplies per written instructions on the board.
- Introduce yourself and describe both professional you and personal you. Remember you want to be seen as a person as well as an authority figure. Use humor and share stories that they can relate to you.

    (One of us begins each school year with a story about a math teacher whom we have chosen to leave nameless. The story would include how each morning this particular woman would be hunched over her overhead projector and look at the class by looking over the tops of her glasses, which, by the way, usually sat at the end of her nose. Each lesson was the same. She presented the material, gave one or two examples on the overhead, and concluded her teaching with asking if there were any questions.

If there were any students who were brave enough to raise their hands, her response would begin by explaining that had they been listening, they would understand how she determined the correct answer to a set problem. Sharing that there was a reason why this individual was put into one of our lives made the point of the story. This student experience was to remind us of how "not" to teach and what "not to be like as a teacher. The Edutainer realizes that it is important to connect with her students and show empathy. The story is also a wonderful introduction to our expectations, which eventually brings about the class rules.)

- Discuss expectations and most importantly why these expectations are needed. Demonstrate how they affect each of the players in the production and without them how we would all be impacted. Focus on the positives and stress the benefits for all. Have these posted or possibly printed to send home for the parents to review and sign.

- Discuss rules and consequences. Again, focus on the positive and express that the classroom is a community, which is built upon respect and fairness for all. Relate it to the real world in that we all have rights and well as responsibilities. Violators will be prosecuted to protect the innocent and consequences will fit the crimes. Remember, everyone wants to be successful.

- Remind your students that these are ways to help them achieve success and that it can be accomplished very simply. Your attitude and enthusiasm is pivotal for creating an atmosphere of cohesiveness and compassion. Express yourself as a partner who is vested in the success for all.

- Have students get acquainted with the classroom. Explain that everything in the room has a purpose and each of us is responsible for making this classroom function. Discuss the job opportunities introduced in the organization chapter. Explain, model, and encourage how and when each task is to be done. Don't assume anything. Everyone has different standards, and the Edutainer wants to show her students that she has high expectations and what the acceptable standard of performing a task is.

- When students understand how the classroom is run, they are more likely to do what is asked of them. They become more willing to help.

Think about it; when you are at a public place or even a friend's home, if you knew how to help, you would be more apt to do so. The same feelings apply here. Don't teach your students to wait to be asked—teach them to be proactive. Be a member of the community!

- Review the posted daily schedule and have students record it in their agenda if appropriate for your grade level. Otherwise, type the daily schedule and have students take a copy of it home to share with their parents.
- Discuss lunchroom, recess, and snack times. Be sure to include expected behavior both in and outside of the classroom, for example, in the halls or on campus grounds.
- Discuss morning and afternoon routines and procedures. Be clear about who is dismissing the class and how students will move from the door to the desk. Include proper times to sharpen pencils, get materials from cubbies or lockers. In the past, we have often used the analogy of sharpening a pencil to that of running a vacuum cleaner. How would the students feel if they were talking or asking a question and the teacher began sharpening her pencil? Stress how difficult it is hear the lesson or directions if you're not present in the room.
- Save bathroom or water breaks for when the teacher isn't presenting or sharing information. Humor makes some of this dry content a bit more tolerable and certainly more memorable in place of just moving from one rule to the next.
- Discuss proper procedures for arriving tardy to school or what to do if absent. Again, stress student responsibility, not parent or teacher. Every day from the first determines how students will behave and what will be expected from them.
- Vary activities. Obviously the first day requires the teacher to do much of the talking, but try to give students an opportunity to do something other than just sitting and listening. See some of the intermission activities or share some fun activities that have to do with them listening and writing.
- Send home student questionnaire to be completed by parents (see parent questionnaire).
- Any type of afternoon or dismissal routine needs to begin today. Explain how the class is to be dismissed from students, their belongings, assignments, and preparations for tomorrow. Stress the idea that no one leaves until the entire class is ready. Younger students in tables or assigned to types of jobs can be announced to gather first as to eliminate mass scrambling during dismissal. Others can be dismissed by location

of room or possibly school responsibilities, for example, clubs, safety guards, and so forth. Again, this isn't going to happen perfectly on the first day. As the Edutainer, you are in control and there to guide what is working and what needs a "retake."

First Few Days and Weeks of School: Scene 1, Take 2

You have introduced and established yourself as the director and have welcomed your cast onto the stage of learning. Therefore, leading roles as well as supporting roles have been assigned. Now they must be rehearsed and practiced. Expectations are understood and rules must now be enforced. Routines and procedures need to become front-and-center daily activities. Every year so many teachers are in such an incredible hurry to get to chapter 1 in each of their curriculums yet never bother to explain how or why students are to achieve success.

Unfortunately, these are the very classrooms that are still explaining mid-year what the Edutainer taught in the first month, only they work with a group of students who never became connected in the ideas of responsibility and accountability as a class. These teachers have taught their students to be reactive instead of proactive.

The Edutainer chooses to work in the motion of moving forward with goals versus tracking backward with regrets and threats. As you ease into the textbooks and daily assignments, keep these ideas in mind; most importantly, plan to make them a daily practice that is modeled by you and your students. Make time each day to explain and rehearse expectations, rules, and procedures.

- *Review student interactions.* Move students or rearrange desks if behavior problems begin or movement in the classroom isn't flowing as well as you had hoped it would. Discuss voice volume that is used inside vs. outside. Review appropriate times to leave seats and when specific materials are needed. Review schedule. Get your students to begin to think for themselves about the daily lessons and the order of the books that they use.
- *Be center stage.* Use body language when addressing poor behavior. Move around the room and respond quickly when rules are broken with consequences that were discussed as a class. Orally review work that is given in the first few days to allow students to see what is expected and accepted. Be aware of which students are successfully performing and which students are already struggling or possibly not even completing

assignments. Look for opportunities to praise students and opportunities to offer helpful suggestions.

- *Consider developing a pattern of morning work.* Are your students old enough to enter the classroom and settle into a morning routine without being assigned something to do, or do you need to supply a small task (sponge activity) to possibly develop some study skills as well as establish a productive morning ritual? Journaling, proofreading, summarizing, reviewing, or comprehending a previous or upcoming topic are great ideas to get the mind going. These ten or fifteen minutes that begin each morning set the tone for the rest of the day. The Edutainer should not be a babysitter minding each movement or conversation of every student until a formal announcement or school broadcast appears to quiet the classroom.

- *Students do need to be reminded to perform the following routines until they are established.* Make this a morning plan with you as the facilitator until the students are completing these behaviors in an acceptable and timely fashion, and, most important, independently. The classroom should be in control at all times. With students arriving at different times there will be movement but not mutiny. Most important, the students understand what is expected of them. Morning routines might include the following:
  - Unstacking chair and putting under assigned desk
  - Writing daily assignments or announcements in agenda or set place in notebook—teacher checks everyday to reinforce the importance
  - Independent reading of a chosen book for monthly book report or reading log
  - Turning in work for the day or at the very least locating it in folder/binder
  - Unpacking belongings, tidying desk or cubby/locker
  - Sharpening pencils, having paper for the day
  - Getting ahead with weekly assignments possibly from spelling, writing, or vocabulary drill workbooks
  - Remind students to check teacher class page on Internet if this is a choice for a communication tool; use a neat question or fun icon to find as an incentive for becoming self-sufficient learners

- *Discuss expectations of students completing class work.* Are students allowed to whisper or ask other students for help? What are they to do if they need help from you? Many teachers use systems that signal to the teacher that they need help. For example, turning a plastic cup up on their desk to symbolize information needing to go into the cup. Otherwise the cup is placed in a downward position where the opening is flat against the desk. Are the students to raise their hand or would you like them to come up to you?

- *Orally review and check appropriate headings of papers, neatness, and use of spacing.* Model correct and incorrect examples. As a class, discuss how the paper needs to be made acceptable. Is print or cursive expected? Do students write on the front and back of a paper? Did you notice the margins on the paper? Use them. Save the "wave motion" for sporting events. Don't wait until students become comfortable with bad habits. Just as a coach wouldn't watch his batter swing incorrectly time after time without correcting the hand or swing position, the Edutainer models, and corrects what she witnesses, day to day. Be active and alert with every routine that is expected. Make this a part of plans for each lesson.
- *Share expectations of student behavior when teacher is speaking.* Are the students allowed to leave their seats? Do they need to wait until you are done presenting an idea or can they ask a question as it arises? Are they supposed to be following along if you're reading from a text? Should students jot down main ideas or fill in study sheets while the lesson is presented? All of these behaviors need to be addressed. Don't assume students will exhibit appropriate behavior until it has been taught. Yes, this is part of the curriculum; it is called learning.
- *Discuss expectations of student behavior when other students are presenting.* Students need to learn how to actively listen when others are speaking. Listening skills are just as important as speaking skills. It is important to model both. These directions are just as important as the actual assignment that the students will be sharing. Plan for this with the same attention and detail that you would for the rubric that you will be using to determine grades.
- *Discuss policy of late work and absent work.* Model where the student is to check for missed assignments and where to return them when complete (see Absent Sheet in the appendix, page 167). Discuss where late work is returned and how it is graded. Again, rules have been established. Now students need to see these rules in action. Many teachers use the buddy system.
- *When a student is absent,* he has another student to rely on for getting his work or at the very least able to call him from home. We like the idea of the absent folder, as discussed in the organization chapter. Here, each student has a separate folder with his name on it in an absent box. When the teacher is passing out handouts or even tests, she can simply

put these papers in the folder so when the student returns, all handouts are already there. Depending on the age of the students, a weekly job can be assigned to handle these absent students, too.

- *Class reward systems should also be discussed during these days.* Incentives, whether on an individual basis or classroom system, need to be understood and implemented. We have found that parents are wonderful about supplying rewards, as their children get excited about the opportunity to earn them and ultimately are the recipients of their generosity.
- *Explain, model, and practice daily traffic patterns, transition times, and dismissal times.* Don't let a day go by that students don't hear you say and practice expectations for these behaviors. Discuss and model the idea of time management; think aloud and share strategies with students about using time wisely and getting ahead throughout the day and week. What are students to do if they do not finish an assignment though they were given ample time to do so? These activities are the very core of classroom learning. The idea of a community is built over time and practiced daily.

Best Supporting Role
Enter the substitute folder. There will be days that you plan to be away from your class and other days that are planned for you. Either way, the Edutainer is prepared for both expected and unexpected days of being away from the stage. The substitute folder is a simple way of saving some good scripts for the stand-in. Your school might require a certain binder and provide you a list of items that the folder should include. If you are not provided any information, the following suggestions will provide a wonderful peace of mind to all parties involved (see Substitute Folder Checklist in the appendix, page 168).

- Map of school
- Daily schedule, which includes times, lessons, and classroom locations
- Teachers that teach on your team and/or resource teachers that your students report to for special or elective classes
- Helpful students from each class
- Seating charts for each class
- Lesson plans, both specific for expected absences and generic for unexpected absences, that fit into the curriculum; to avoid any confusion, house all generic plans in a separate folder
- Textbooks, especially teacher editions, should the substitute need help with the answers

- Worksheets or any other manipulatives that are used for the lesson
- Emergency procedures, for example, fire or tornado drill
- Additional information for special needs students
- Brief description of your classroom management plan, daily routines, and travel routes to and from other rooms throughout the day, for example, library, lunchroom, bathrooms, and so forth
- Ask the substitute to make comments about the lessons. Did the students finish? Did the students struggle with any of the content? Were there any behavior problems that you need to be aware of? Were papers graded and/or collected?

The substitute folder if done correctly can be used year after year. It remains the same with the exception of current lesson plans and obviously the schedule and students of the designated year. Now that you, the effective teacher, are prepared for the day of being away from your classroom, your students need to be as well. The Edutainer rehearses expectations and assures students that if the community is prepared for transitions, its members and practices will be just fine.

Lesson Planning: Scripts, Schedules, and Standards

A good teacher, like a good entertainer first must hold his audience's attention; then he can teach his lesson.

—John Henrik Clarke

Enter the idea of an effective teacher actually planning meaningful lessons in a well-managed classroom. A tall order? Absolutely, but the Edutainer has established her community and built relationships with her students by incorporating responsibility and accountability. So how does an effective teacher determine what to plan, how to plan, and know how much to plan? We don't attempt here to provide lesson plans for anyone.

However, considering our vast amount of experience with both public and private education, not to mention experience from first grade to college, we thought we could give you some suggestions as to what to consider before simply opening a text and beginning with chapter 1.

Yearly Scope and Sequence
Just as you teach your students to become familiar with their texts, you as the teacher must do the same. Why? In the twenty-first century we are not short

on knowledge as it is only a "click" away but rather we are short on time and effective applications in the classroom. Simply put, the textbook is only a tool that the effective teacher uses.

- Before any planning can take place, the effective teacher must first know the standards for the grade level that she is teaching. The National Standards and State Standards allow for correct pacing and spiraling of content to avoid gaps and overlaps and teachers determining their own curriculum. We all have our opinions as to what is really important and necessary, but these agreed upon goals and objectives keep us all on the same page. We live in a global society and must agree on what is appropriate learning for each age during formal education, so there is no child left behind.
- Curriculum must then be selected that develops these strands of concepts and incorporates activities and assessments.
- The effective teacher must determine exactly what and how these ideas are to be used in the classroom. This approach is commonly referred to as curriculum mapping. Ideally, a school would determine time for each grade level to do this together as it promotes consistency between teachers that share a common age of students and a unified approach as to what information will be taught, when it will be taught, and finally how long it will be taught. This is not to suggest that teachers will not have their own ideas or methodologies used in individual classrooms, but it would create some directions as to what each semester or quarter would cover.
- Think about it this way, curriculum mapping merely provides some parameters for the teachers. It aligns the curriculum in graphing terms both horizontally and vertically. You have "this much material to cover" and "this much time" to get it done. How you choose to present it and make it relevant to the students is up to you. There is plenty of room for creativity and teacher individuality. This time and effort put forth in planning comes back in spades. It can be used year after year and tweaked the second time around as experience teaches what ideas worked and did not work.
- Differentiated instruction must then be considered. All students do not come packaged with the same ability levels. Good planning allows for on-level learning, remediation, and enrichment activities. Here, you must think about whether the texts and activities suggested are enough for a variety of levels. Do you need to purchase extra workbooks, Google other ideas, or come up with some of your own?

- Finally, what type of assessments will you use to determine how your students' understanding and performance will be measured? Use a variety of instruments such as daily work, quizzes, tests, and student-created work. How many grades will be needed during a particular grading period? Your grading policy should be consistent with teammates and the grades both above and below the one you are teaching. Are monthly reports or projects a consideration? If so, they need to be implanted ahead of time. Verbal and written should be included. Be careful with ideas such as student participation and group grades. Both can be a bit challenging when it comes to grading individual work instead of personality and behavioral attributes.

Daily Lesson

Now that you have a handle on what information needs to be covered and the amount of time allotted, the effective teacher must turn her attention to everyday planning. This can be especially intimidating if you are assigned a variety of subjects every day, as in the elementary classroom. Again, this book does not attempt to provide an iron-clad plan for all but instead provides suggestions that need to be considered when making individual plans. Consider the following.

- Remember, kids have short attention spans, and you need to keep this in mind as you plan. As Mary Domino explains, "Today, a short attention span can be attributed to the fact that our brains are trained in short sound bytes and video clips. Think about it, when we watch TV, we are inundated with hundreds of images a minute. And TV is quick; a lot of flash with sometimes very little content. Watching TV can be hypnotizing in its effect—mindless, almost mind numbing. All that, along with having access to text, Internet, media, and email in the phone that is in the palm of our hands makes us overstimulated with nonsense and under-stimulated mentally at the same time. A huge dilemma that can leave a person unfulfilled yet feeling very busy, too busy for getting anything done."
- Take and make notes. When you prepare for a lesson, study the chapter ahead of the students. Refamiliarize yourself with these concepts, so you can make the connections needed between individual concepts. Write on sticky notes and actually place them in your book. These will be helpful if you get off track or forget something you wanted to add to the topic. Be able to paraphrase the information into conversational or storyline style.

- Use graphic organizers for presenting notes to your class, or have students use them while discussing the lesson (see the appendix for forms, pages 169–75). Use these aids to teach study skills such as note taking, outlining, or simply chunking information into smaller more meaningful pieces.
- Differentiate activities throughout the lesson. Objectives should involve teacher- and student-centered activities. Consider the different needs of the auditory, visual, and kinesthetic learners.
- Encourage opportunities for students to connect or personalize the lesson. Motivate students to see how the information affects them and how it is applicable to the real world. Without this association, the information is only here today but gone tomorrow. Students must be expected to do something with the material instead of simply memorizing it.
- Plan to teach and practice opportunities that reinforce class expectations, rules, and daily routines.
- Maximize all academic time. Always plan for more than you expect to finish in a given lesson.
- Be flexible. Some lessons will be brilliant; others will have to be revised or simply discarded. Be prepared to work off the top of your head, too.
- Contrary to popular opinion, especially among students, homework is a necessary evil. Why? It is a task that reinforces accountability, responsibility, and an opportunity to strengthen study skills. Students do not advance to higher level or enriched classes without the ability to work independently. The Edutainer only assigns relevant work not busy work. Encourage your students to develop study cards from assignments, handouts, notes, and texts, and actually read the text instead of just scanning for answers.

Every solid lesson has a beginning, middle, and an end, and the session should flow from one part to the next. Introductions should state the objective. These goals should be achieved through meaningful and personal teacher and student connections. Finally, the student's understanding must be evaluated in terms that could be as informal as a quick oral group review or as formal as an individual test. The effective teacher uses her discernment as to what is necessary and appropriate. From the first act to the closing of the curtain, no class is left to chance. Preparation is key for an award-winning production.

SCENE 4

Organization

Organizing is what you do before you do something, so that when you do it, it is not all mixed up.

—A. A. Milne (creator of Winnie the Pooh)

This chapter is designed to remind all of the veteran teachers who diligently return to their assigned classrooms the following fall or the new, just beginning educators who are still able to recall, on demand, all of Bloom's levels of taxonomy, just how the upcoming year gets started. For those of us returning, you can relate to walking into the room and seeing such a disarray of furniture and the settled dust of the past two months not to mention that feeling that desperately overwhelms you of "Where do I begin?"

Or perhaps the novice entering the newly assigned stage for the very first time thinking, "This is all mine, yet I'm not sure where to get started." Just as you the teacher must make some order of the classroom before taking on any planning, the student must make sense of the physical surroundings before owning any of the learning aspects.

Setting the Stage

Setting up the classroom is one of the most important tasks that a teacher can do because it determines what kind of learning will be done in the classroom, and it establishes daily routines. Desk placements, availability of sup-

73

plies, and daily schedules, as well as student and teacher resources, are just a few of the physical characteristics of a well-organized room.

An Edutainer maintains a classroom that is neat, organized, and, most important, produces a predictable routine that is witnessed when observing its cast, the students. This setting is an environment that fosters cohesiveness and productivity. This chapter is designed to help you better organize the space, materials, and students in your classroom, so you can effectively manage all important elements of a successful production while both on and off stage.

There are two points to consider with organization. First, most of these strategies are designed for K–6 grades, due to the needs of the students. However, many of the strategies are applicable to older grade levels as well, especially the organization of materials and space. The second point is to be realistic about your own organization skills. Many think of organization as an art or a gift that some people have and some people don't have.

We see two extremes in the dos and the don'ts, which we would group as the OCDs and the SLOBs. If you are obsessive then you may spend all summer organizing your classroom and materials, to the point a surgery could be performed in the room, and still feel the need to do more. On the other hand, you may feel overwhelmed initially with the whole organizing venture because it's just not your "thing." This is the person who has so many wrappers on the car floorboard that you haven't actually seen the floorboard in two years—or your bedroom looks like a clothing display table at Ann Taylor if they had a 75 percent off sale.

So for the OCD, relax, follow our strategies and then move on. For the SLOB, breathe deep . . . relax . . . now take one strategy at a time and slowly make your way through them until you can actually see the semblance of a classroom (hint: it shouldn't look like your car interior). Remember, organization is essential to preparing for a year of learning that is relaxed, enjoyable, and productive. Now let's get started!

Desk Placement

Did you know that a teacher's discipline problems are often directly proportional to the distance she maintains from her students? Think about it; the farther the teacher stands from her students the more distance there is

> DID YOU KNOW . . . We typically only use only 20 percent of what we keep. The other 80 percent is stored and sits and sits. . . . No wonder we need to organize.

between the two. Consequently, students in the back of the room acquire more opportunity to become removed or bored—eventually leading them to less desirable behavior.

While there is no one correct way to arrange a classroom, you have to take your teaching style into consideration. Is the delivery of instruction mainly teacher-centered or student-centered? Usually, the younger the student, the closer the desk pattern, as the older student needs a bit more room. Students' desks are traditionally set in straight rows, or sets of two or three desks. Small groups of four or six desks can also be utilized. One thing you might want to remember is that when the Edutainer isn't on stage, the students in groups of four or six can become focused on or entertained by those immediately at their table.

We personally like the idea of the "U" design. Interestingly, the U-shape is similar to the design of seating around a stage. The teacher's desk is diagonally placed in the front right side of the room. A "teaching table" is placed

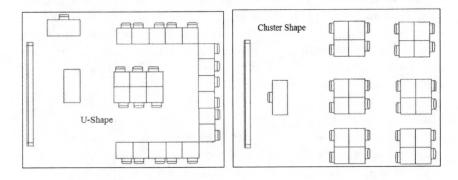

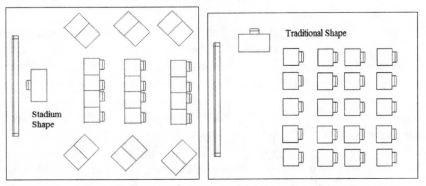

Figure 4.1.

in the front of the room right in the middle of the "U." This is a small table where all handouts, teaching editions, and materials are kept to allow for quick transitions between lessons. Think of it as a working area for daily plans and resources needed in the order of their presentation. Each can be color-coded or tabbed, so the pages can be referenced quickly.

The Edutainer is always prepared and has her "lines and roles" at her fingertips. The students' desks are then arranged either in a large single shape "U," or they can be arranged in a small "U" within a larger shaped "U." Both the teacher and students can move about freely to other areas of the room, enter and leave the room, and the desks can even be arranged quickly to small tables of four or five desks. Ultimately no desk is hidden from any view in the room. Refer to common desk arrangement diagrams as shown in figure 4.1. The best scenario for the placement of desks allows for an area where students can get on the floor when working with partners and when reading independently or being read to by the teacher.

Finally students should be assigned seating to maximize learning and minimize any behavioral issues once you become familiar with your students. It is also an easy and quick way to learn the students' names. As far as the first day of school is concerned, alphabetical order or students with special needs can be used until you are familiar with all of the students' faces and names. (Refer to name game in intermission 2.)

Learning Centers

A learning center is an area designed to encourage student activity and choice during specific times. They can be used to meet specific learning objectives, or they can be used to motivate, reinforce, and support projects for particular content areas. Learning centers are also valuable because they can be structured or allow students freedom of choice and motivate students to pursue personal interests.

For example, an interest center focused on encouraging students to read for pleasure and for information of personal interest might contain books chosen by the students. The student choosing the book puts a bookmark in it explaining why she chose it for the learning center. Most elementary classrooms have interest centers, such as a reading corner, a game area, or a science center. Middle and high school classrooms might set up such centers for current events or reading materials related to the subject area.

One benefit of learning centers is that the students have more physical space in which to work rather than confinement to a desk. Remember, we are talking about children who are active and full of energy; sometimes they just have to move around the room and get out from behind their desks.

There was a fourth-grade teacher in our school who was fortunate to have been chosen as the recipient of a project constructed by an Eagle Scout. The project he chose to construct was a castle for the classroom. The castle took up a large section of the room, but its usefulness far outweighed the space it took up. It had room in the bottom and on top for beanbag chairs and throw pillows, so it was perfect for a reading center. It also served as the stage from which the students presented their book talks and other projects as they stood in the castle tower and gave their performances. Puppet shows were video taped and enjoyed by both students and parents alike.

While it may not be feasible for every teacher to have a castle in her room, it does show unique ways that learning centers can be set up to make the educational process fun and exciting! Who knows—maybe there is an Eagle Scout in your school looking for a project to build?

Supplies

As long as there are students in a classroom, there will be a great demand for supplies. And these materials have to be accessible. There is something to be said for the old saying "I'll get the first one for you, and then you're on your own." Remember, the Edutainer encourages student responsibility versus teacher dependency. The same idea applies to the classroom supply center. The Edutainer displays her materials or props in a neat and orderly fashion—most importantly in a manner that is easily labeled and obtainable by the student.

We also believe that getting up to get supplies every time an assignment is given can take up valuable instructional time. Therefore, students should have a supply of lined paper, and a pencil box filled with several sharpened pencils at his desk. Red pencils are great to have on hand, too. They can be used to self-evaluate or peer-edit assignments. An extra eraser and an assortment of colored pencils and/or crayons might also be a wise choice. Students can then visit the supply center, which is described next, on an as-needed basis rather than an hourly one to replenish or replace necessary tools.

The student supply center (see figure 4.2) is simply an area or table that holds everyday materials. Lined paper, white paper, and construction paper are displayed in separate colors using simple metal in and out bins or cardboard file boxes (mailboxes) purchased from a local office or school supply store. Plastic boxes consisting of drawers that hold pencils, sharpeners, tape, staples, and highlighters can be included, too. Pencil sharpeners, staplers, and a three-ring hole puncher are placed on top of the table. Depending on the age of the students some of these supplies can be deleted or replaced with others.

Figure 4.2.

The whole idea behind this center is that students are responsible for getting their own supplies and have a neat and orderly place for storage. Most teachers create student supply lists or teacher "wish lists" in the beginning of the year. These supplies are stored in cabinets or boxes depending upon the school and then brought out as needed to refresh the center. Finally, baskets of white boards, expo markers, and erasers or simply tissue can be stored here, too. The Edutainer uses white boards while practicing a lesson so her student is "actively" listening and practicing during a whole group instruction (refer to the Student Supply List in the appendix, page 176).

Collecting Assignments

The other part of the student supply center is a place where assignments are returned. Again, here is the idea of the "in and out bins," labeled for each subject area in an assignment bin (see figure 4.3). One common practice that is used in many schools is the idea of assigning a student a number. When papers are collected, the student assigned with "checking documents" can easily arrange the papers in numerical order and determine which student did not turn in a particular assignment. This ordering of papers makes it very easy to record grades and know what assignments are missing, too. A separate slot is also assigned for late and then make-up work. Handling these papers will be discussed later in the management chapter.

Backpacks/Coats/Extra Shoes

These items are the very things that can make or break the space factor or path of travel in a classroom. One jacket or backpack in the middle of the floor, especially near the door, can cause utter bedlam in a just a few minutes. As a result students should be assigned a space or possible locker/cubby with their names or assigned numbers. Plastic crates can also be utilized and stacked on top of each other. If every desk, allotted space, and/or cubby is labeled with the student's name or simply numbered with his assigned number, think about how easy it is to locate that child's books, binders, and other supplies.

For example, when a child is absent and a parent requests make-up work or a child is being checked out early, or better yet, unexpectedly, you can have another student grab his books while you're jotting down any assigned reading or work. All of this can be sent to the front office in a matter of

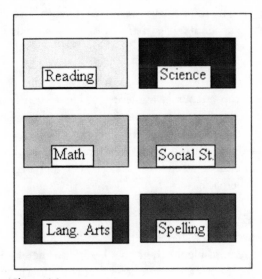

Figure 4.3.

minutes. You talk about being able to do something quickly; this is it! It's handled and done. No more waiting until your planning time or gathering these requests after school. Organization prevents procrastination and stress in a big way.

Classroom Library

Reading is imperative when it comes to improving students' vocabulary and writing skills. When a child enters the early elementary years, he is learning "how to read." However, the older elementary child (typically fourth grade) and beyond is reading "to learn." Therefore a student must be given time throughout the day to simply read. Many elementary teachers are familiar with the acronym "DEAR Time," or "Drop Everything And Read." It is not enough to hope that students will find the right book or begin to enjoy reading by assigning book reports or even visiting the media center on a weekly basis. A variety of genres should be accessible for a particular grade level.

The classroom library can be as simple as a set of shelving, which can easily be color-coded using the very dots that can be purchased for retail tags or even garage sales. We suggest including a variety of literature that represents the following genres: realistic fiction, historical fiction, science fiction, autobiographical and biographical narratives, fantasy, sports, mystery, poetry, and even hobbies such as drawing or "how to books."

For example, all historical fiction would have a red dot on the spine of the book, whereas realistic fiction might all be coded using the green dots. Students will also need a "check out list" including the date, name of the student and book, and the date the book was returned (refer to "See a Book, Check It Out" Sheet in the appendix, page 177). A handy sign including the types of genres with an assigned colored dot should be displayed close to the library, so that students can easily identify what books are from what genre (refer to "How Do I Find a Kind of Book?" Sheet in the appendix, page 178).

New teachers can encourage students to donate gently used books and even purchase used books at local library book sales. Retailers have become quite savvy with this idea as well. Teachers can obtain a ten to fifteen percent discount with valid school identification at national bookstores. Going online is a great resource, too. Used books can be purchased for next to nothing, especially paperbacks.

Resource Materials

As we mentioned earlier, older elementary and junior high students are becoming more responsible for their own learning. Therefore they will have different needs for the necessary resources that will allow them to help themselves independently. These resources might include dictionaries, thesauri, specific novels or selected stories for literature circles, and even atlases, or drawing books, which could encourage hesitant writers.

Technology resources such as laptops or even jump drives could be included. Nonetheless, all resources are shared and need to be stored in a neat and accessible fashion. A true Edutainer understands that these resources not only need to be available to her students but also introduced and modeled. She wouldn't expect her students to be able to include them in their performance without a proper rehearsal.

Classroom Responsibilities or Jobs

One quote that has become quite famous and that is very accurate for the active classroom is "It takes a village." The Edutainer must assign all of the players' roles. Once your classroom is organized and set up, it must remain that way for the entire year. Most importantly, the students must understand, practice, and ultimately "own" their responsibilities while establishing a sense of community. This is where the director role comes into play. All of the students' names are written on a colorful picture of a pencil, for example, and these surround a decorative folder that is labeled "Weekly Classroom Assignments." Smaller colorful pictures of notebooks or pieces of paper list various jobs.

Each week the director assigns her cast new roles to perform by simply retrieving a new name from a box each week and rotating the student who was assigned job 1 to job 2. By the end of the school year, each student will have the opportunity to perform each role at least once, if not twice. You'll be surprised how much the students enjoy being a cast member and holding each other responsible for their own tasks. We suggest the following tasks assignments in table 4.1.

Classroom Wall Organization

The walls of a classroom should serve two purposes. One is to display work and the other to share instructional information. Displaying work is easy. Nowadays, there are so many ideas that can be borrowed to display assignments that celebrate seasons, concepts, or simply award-winning performances. These can be purchased from local school stores, which include the colorful and thematic icons, or they can simply be downloaded from the wealth of other teachers' websites or online magazines. In any event, an art or advertising degree is not required.

Table 4.1. Task Assignments

Task Assignments	
√ Date √ Distribution of handouts/weekly Friday folders √ Document checker—numbers, alphabetizes, and files returning folders √ P.M. person—handles trash/floor duty √ Student supply center √ Resources √ Library √ A.M. person—prepares for school broadcast of announcements that requires media to be turned on √ Messenger √ Attendance	√ Job supervisor—checks to see that all players are performing their assigned roles and can even change the chart on Friday for the following week √ Manager of weekly store (to be discussed later) √ Lights √ Monitor/recess equipment—reports behavior when in halls and transitioning from class to class and carries any class equipment both to and from the play area

If you are fortunate to have your own or a shared assistant, this is a great opportunity to receive some additional help. The second purpose of the classroom wall is to inform students of how the class operates. The Edutainer utilizes several key components before her first act even begins.

Daily Schedule

This can be created using a hanging set of pockets commonly referred to as "teacher pocket pal," which can be purchased from a school supply store (see figure 4.4). The top row of pockets simply lists the days of the week beginning with Monday using colored index cards. The underlying pockets list the daily schedule in a vertical fashion using the same color of that day.

For example, Monday is written on a bright yellow index card. Underneath the day of the week, students can see a listing of all yellow cards that begins with homeroom or morning work and ends with the final center/class or activity for the day. You'll never have to endure another "What are we doing today?" question again. Promise!

Bulletin Boards

These are great opportunities that advertise a display for "What do I do during morning time or homeroom?" Again, the local school store sells neat little packages of thematic ideas or decorations shaped like academic supplies such as pencils or erasers or leaves for autumn (see figure 4.5).

The Edutainer suggests the following:

- Unpack backpack
- Locate work that was completed and due today

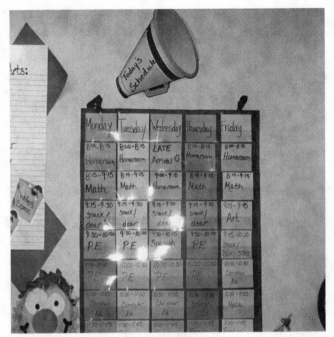

Figure 4.4.

- Read
- Get ahead
- Organize desk/cubby
- Unclutter binder or notebooks
- Record daily assignments for today's agenda (to be discussed in the following paragraph)
- Sharpen pencils
- Be sure to have clean lined paper, etc.

You'll have to adjust these suggestions to the appropriate grade level that you are teaching. This section of the bulletin board remains up all year long to encourage student responsibility and skills that demonstrate proactive behavior. The same can be done for afternoon or dismissal time. Key reminders would include checking to see that all written assignments are recorded in the student's agenda, gathering supplies that will be needed to complete the tasks—not taking every textbook home each night—and finally checking to see that the student's work area is clean and ready to use the following morning.

These are daily routines that need to be not only heard but also seen both at morning and afternoon times. Practice makes a consistent routine. The

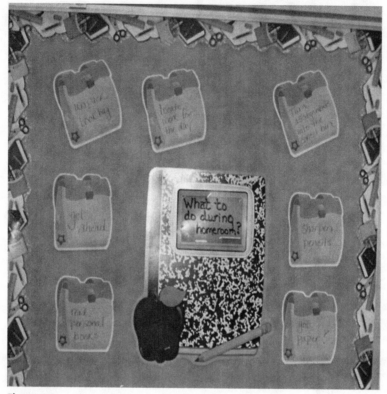

Figure 4.5.

Edutainer wants to model these skills in the beginning of the year but instills them within her students before long.

Certain informational bulletin boards can be designed for the first few weeks of school to help students in the upper elementary grades through middle school get basic information about school life, including a map of the school, classroom rules, the daily schedule, assignment of lockers, lunch prices, and menus. They can also include bus schedules, morning and afternoon pickup locations, and location of carpool. When students are asked at the beginning of the year what concerns they have, their responses invari-

---

DID YOU KNOW . . . It takes twenty-one days to form a new habit. Habits can be good or bad, so let's focus on creating good habits.

ably relate to basic routines, schedules, and locations of important places such as restrooms, lunchroom, lockers, and other classrooms.

Providing this information in a visual format helps students get information without having to ask you continually! Instructional bulletin boards have great potential to enhance learning. Not only do we take in more information visually than through any of the other senses, we also have a much greater capacity for long-term memory of pictures—remember, a picture is worth a thousand words. Visuals also guide understanding.

Think of trying to understand the water cycle, the structure of a flower, or even the layout of the school building without the aid of a visual. Map out the major curricular units you teach during the year. Think about the types of visual displays most effective for each unit. Consider the amount of teacher and student time required to make each display, the materials needed, and the instructional value of each display.

Planning ahead helps you make better use of materials and your time in preparing displays. This is especially important when making a list before heading to the local school supply store in August. Nothing is more overwhelming than walking the crowded aisles with an assortment of everything that was ever made for "educational decorating" with fifty other bewildered shoppers.

How many times have you unloaded your purchases back in your classroom only to think, "What *was* I thinking?" The items were cute and looked interesting in the store, but do you have a place or, better yet, an idea as to how you would use them? So continuing with the spirit of organization, spend some time sifting over your texts before beginning that annual fall shopping spree. What concepts or ideas are presented in your curriculum? If you do not study plants, why purchase the fuzzy plant puzzle explaining the stages of photosynthesis for it only to store dust all year long? Make a list that could be broken down as such:

- Possible themes to consider
- Areas of my curriculum that could use extra practice such as workbooks or extra study guidelines
- Creative posters that you could write rules, schedules, beginning of the year info, etc.
- Calendars or labels for centers or areas
- Objects used to organize such as bins, cubes, trays, etc.
- Bulletin board accessories
- Filing supplies
- Miscellaneous grade and lesson books, stickers, pens, pencils, markers

Agenda or Written Daily Assignments

Designate a part of your white board or purchase a smaller one that will be used to record assignments, tests, projects, or any upcoming special things to know. Purchase colorful rubber tape to section off the days of Monday through Friday that will be written across the top of the board. Again, using the tape, divide each day into subjects or classes with a special miscellaneous area to include extra reminders or upcoming events (see table 4.2).

Each day record all assignments both in and outside of class on the day that the work is actually due. Require your students to copy this daily! Use the idea of a calendar. You wouldn't write down a dentist appointment on Tuesday if it were scheduled on Wednesday. Make this as much like real life as possible. Depending on your school system, students may be assigned a school agenda, or you can simply require a small notebook in which only this information is recorded. Handouts could be made and copied, too. This enforces the idea that we all record the same information in the exact same way (refer to Daily Homework Log in the appendix, page 179).

Other neat benefits that this board offers is that it is a written display of a week's worth of work, and it isn't erased until the following week. If a student is absent, he can see what assignments he missed earlier that week without asking you. It also announces upcoming tests and projects. Just as the Edutainer would not leave her set without knowing what was expected of her the following day, the entire cast is held to this requirement. Tomorrow's act I will be here before you know it. Before we leave this segment on wall organization, let's examine the following guidelines to develop a rich visual environment in your classroom; remember, it is an important part of the stage.

- Use short titles that convey the major intent of the display. Use initial capitals and lowercase letters for titles because students read these much more easily than words in all capitals.

Table 4.2. Agenda

Subject	Mon	Tues	Wed	Thurs	Fri
Reading					
Math					
Science					
Social Studies					
Language Arts					
Spelling					
Don't Forget					

- Choose a common letter style that matches the typeface students see in their print materials, rather than using very decorative letter cutouts. Save creativity for other areas.
- Design bulletin boards to be focused on the intended topic. Don't make them so busy or chaotic that the students have difficulty focusing on essential information, otherwise known as too much "eye candy."
- Choose a background color that provides a sharp contrast between the background and the items placed on it. If the area is poorly lighted, choose light-colored backgrounds. If the area is well lit, then use dark backgrounds.
- Include bulletin boards that students either create or on which they have the option to display their own work. Let them perform, and they will feel ownership in the process.

File, Don't Pile

There are two kinds of filing systems that are used in the elementary and junior high schools. One involves teacher resources, and the other involves students' work. Let's talk about the teacher system first. Separate file cabinets would be ideal when it comes to labeling each drawer as a specific subject. However, if your space is more limited, then simply use color-coded hanging files and regular files within each. For example, in the math drawer or a green hanging folder, you would file individual green folders with labels such as "Chapter 1" or preferably "Place Value," "Rounding," and so forth.

An individual file labeled with just a chapter number can be difficult to reuse when the curriculum is changed and new textbooks are ordered. Your files might not match up. Try to group similar concepts with the same color files. We also like the idea of a "General" drawer. This is a great place to store future lists, conference materials, holiday ideas or handouts, professional observations, credits, and so forth.

Once your files are established, you then have to think about how you are going to get all of the handouts and materials used each day into the system. Don't procrastinate and think, "Oh, I'll file everything I used this week on Friday." For some reason, Friday filing just doesn't seem to happen. What does end up happening is a mound of papers that becomes too big a pile to handle, so it ultimately gets filed in file 13, otherwise known as the trash bin. Instead of putting off the inevitable, the effective teacher keeps a running or open file on her teaching table.

Again, this is a table where she can quickly reference texts, handouts, and other materials that will need to be filed. The "running or open" file can instantly catch materials that were used that day. Once the topic or chapter is completed, it can easily be filed in the permanent system.

The second type of filing system refers to the students' papers. This requires a completely separate crate or file drawer, as it will be used to file everything that the students have completed, that you have graded, or that simply serves as a means of communication such as a notice of a field trip or upcoming conference day. Again, if you are short on room or do not have an abundance of filing drawers, then use a plastic crate. Fill it with hanging folders, one for each student. Label and record the number of the students as we previously discussed, and alphabetize accordingly.

As you grade papers have a bin or crate that serves as a holding file for these. Then every other day or every day, if you are fortunate enough to have an assistant or volunteer, simply drop the papers into the appropriate file.

If you choose to communicate weekly or every other week, the papers are ready to go. We like the idea of a weekly cover letter (see Weekly Cover Letter Handout in the appendix, page 180). Each student receives a stapled cover letter that includes the date that the folder was sent home and requires a parent's signature. You can choose whether you want the entire packet returned or just the signed cover letter.

This is an easy way of communicating with the parent and providing work samples throughout the school year. Each student will also need a folder, possibly labeled "Friday Folder," for whatever day the packets will go home. You can also require that the inside of the folder have two pockets. The left side can be labeled "Keep at Home," and the right side can be labeled "Return to School."

Let's say that all of the folders go home on Friday and are returned on Monday. Have the students take the "signed" cover letter out of the folder and return both in separate piles on Monday or, if they are old enough, place them back in the crate as an assigned job. The folders are easily filed back into the appropriate hanging folder, so they can be opened and filled for the following week. The Edutainer knows that she only wants to handle a paper or folder once; time is wasted if she has to shuffle papers from one point of the room to the next. Handle it wisely the first time, and immediately place it where it needs to be.

Work in Progress

Too many times especially in the older grades, students have assignments that are officially "class work" but roll over to the next day. So what happens to these papers at the end of the first day? All too many times, they become lost, and the owner of the work begins at square one the next day when the rest of the group is just about ready to "put the wrap" on it. One way we've managed to avoid this scenario is by utilizing an area called "Work in Progress." Using a crate or bin that houses folders, label one for each child. If you rotate classes, you might want to make all of your homeroom "red" and then your math group "blue." You get the picture.

Then when assignments do not conform so nicely to set schedules, especially like a writing assignment or science lab that involves multiple steps, the student can drop his work in here until the following day. As you can see everything in the Edutainer's world has a time and place. She can't take the risk that something "might" get done. The same idea applies to someone who exercises. Working out or walking requires thinking ahead and having the equipment or necessary clothes. *Make* it happen and more importantly know *when* you are doing something and *how* it will be done.

MIA Organizer
Just when you are up and rolling and everyone appears to be on the same page, somebody has to be absent or check in/out early. Ah, the nerve of him! Life is what is happening when you're busy making plans. We've got just the fix for the absent student. Reserve another crate, or if you haven't exhausted all of your filing cabinets as of yet, save one for this case. Again, create a file folder for each student using his name and assigned number.

When you are "on stage" and using handouts, it is difficult to remember to put aside materials for those not in class. The best way to handle this is to simply pass the materials out as you normally would, and when you reach the empty desk, place the paper in his file instead of on the desk. However, the only requirement for this idea to work is that the Edutainer must teach her missing cast to check the box upon returning. You can do your best in filling this box up, but if the student does not take the initiative to check this file, all of your work has been in vain. We'll discuss establishing and managing routines more in the management chapter. You can do it; we'll show you how it is done.

Materials Storage
Other important areas include bookcases, closed cabinets, bins, and any other storage unit you may have for materials. Placing storage systems near the area where they are used can be a good time saver. Students in all grades can be taught an efficient system to pass out and collect materials, count to be sure all materials have been returned, and replace the materials neatly in their proper containers. This is part of their responsibility and ownership in the performance. Students learn best when they actively participate rather

than just listen or read; effective management of materials is fundamental to a good instructional program. Good lessons involve good materials.

Records Storage

The Edutainer understands the importance of confidentiality. Therefore, a locked filing cabinet is a necessity for the secure storage of student records: report cards, permanent record folders, standardized test results, anecdotal records, grade books, and other records. It is important to keep the key to that cabinet in a secure place and never allow student access to it. Avoid storing anything in that file cabinet that a substitute teacher, parent volunteer, or instructional aide might need.

Because some records may be stored on the computer, the teacher's responsibility also includes ensuring that these records are secure and stored according to school and district policy. While the Edutainer enjoys performing and incorporating the cast into the performance, she is also a professional who understands the litigious nature of our culture.

Benefits of Organization

Now that we have you organized and ready for your opening day act, here are a few ideas that will help you lessen your weekend and evening workload throughout the school year. Remember, you organized your classroom so you won't spend every waking moment there or bring school home with you.

- *Stay late or come in early.* Coming in an hour early once or twice a week can make the difference between a weekend grading projects or exams on your sofa and a weekend watching your favorite episodes of *The Simpsons* . . . we mean *CSI.*
- *Avoid giving tests on Friday.* To reduce your weekend work, stay on top of your paperwork during the week. Rotate due dates, and don't give tests on Fridays if at all possible.
- *Communicate.* We will discuss this in more detail in another chapter, but keep parents in the loop. Be proactive in communicating information and set limits so you aren't overwhelmed. Tell parents, for instance, that you will check messages once a day in the morning or evening or that you only check e-mail once or twice a day. You are in the classroom for the students and with students. The effective teacher does not have a desk job, which lends itself to instantly respond to e-mails as they "pop up" on the computer.

- *Involve your students in classroom tasks.* Remember, part of their responsibility in the classroom is to have jobs and tasks that they perform. This gives them ownership and gives you a break. Let them switch papers and grade quizzes so that you aren't doing all the work. Being an effective leader, you know when you need to grade an assignment or simply orally review it with the class. The Edutainer understands that she can't leave work exhausted every day and return the following day to be an effective teacher.

- *Make time for fun.* Performers need down time. You have to rejuvenate your creativity, and you need rest. If you are organized, then you should free up time for more relaxation. We all need down time away from school. Also take care of your health. You have only one body, so treat it well. Being an Edutainer is not an option if you're absent.

As we leave this section we would like to share a list of benefits of becoming organized.

- Saves time
- Relieves stress
- Provides more space
- Gives good impressions
- You can actually find things when you need them
- You will feel better because you are in control and organized
- Allows for an extra cup of coffee each morning
- You can now focus on your performance

Again, there is no one "right" way to organize or set up a given classroom. Your "stage" is designed correctly if all of the props and scenery allow you, the Edutainer, and your cast to accomplish what you set out to achieve. Just like entertainment, there is no one person who can carry all of the weight of the entire casting crew. Each member has his part and must first understand where everything is before the show can begin. In June, your audience will want an encore if the stage is set, the Edutainer is ready, and the show goes well. "Roll 'em!"

SCENE 5

Management

We are what we repeatedly do. Excellence, therefore, is not an act, but a habit.

—Aristotle

If there were one area of management that is most important to a teacher, especially a new teacher, it would be in the area of classroom management. Studies have identified the lack of discipline as one of the biggest problems in public schools over the past three decades. In fact, one of the major determining factors in the success of a new teacher is not subject knowledge but rather the ability to manage a classroom. Bottom line, whether or not students learn depends upon the teacher's ability to control the classroom.

According to Mary Dimino (2009 Gracie Allen Award–winning comedian), "A teacher, like a stand-up comic, needs to own her stage (i.e., have control of the audience), use her voice to hit vocally certain important key words (punch the punch lines), physically move her body as to act out what she is saying instead of just talking about what she is saying (act-outs), and in the end they need to have likeability, in show business we call this the 'it' factor."

A classroom, however, doesn't become well managed overnight. You have to remember that every fall, excited new students fill a room with an unknown teacher. Therefore, each new year, the "unknown" must spend time teaching the students her expectations, rules, and routines before beginning any academic content.

As Edutainers, we like to go beyond that thinking. Instead of just explaining rules and schedules, the Edutainer first establishes an environment that is built upon respect. We begin with the idea of a community and understand that all players have a role. Each individual is "vested" in the learning experience. Second, the Edutainer builds a relationship, which is nurtured over time with real communication, action, and results. Finally, the Edutainer instills responsibility within the student and holds that expectation as a high standard. Although the Edutainer is the director for setting the management stage, her cast also has a responsibility in this area.

Understand that this is not accomplished on the first day of school, and that yes, you were hired to "teach," but once you establish a safe environment and an atmosphere of respect, the students will have the desire to learn and also know that you believe in them. Whatever time you devote in the beginning of the year will establish and maintain the classroom environment for the rest of the year. So, what kinds of strategies are involved in making all of this happen? And exactly how does the cast learn to contribute to the overall performance while enhancing their own learning? Let's begin with understanding why we do what we do.

We have already established that the effective teacher does not begin the new school year with presenting lessons, handouts, and numerous activities "just to keep the students busy." This is because before long the unmotivated student will tire of the endless assignments and no longer be a part of the learning community. He will naturally want to know "Why do I need to do this?" or claim, "I won't use this in real life."

Some students are motivated to work hard and do their best no matter what is asked of them. Simply put, these individuals have excellent work habits, and their personal success is incentive enough. However, the majority of the students in today's classroom are not wired that way. And the teacher is left determining the incentive for these less motivated learners.

Enter the management system. Did you know that research has suggested that the level of a student's achievement is directly linked to the amount of time that a student spends with his studies? This sounds simple enough; the more you study, the more you know. So, here lies the difference between the successful and unsuccessful performance of the year. The entire cast must be on the same page; ultimately they must believe in the same goals and means and share a common understanding of how they will achieve their results. Otherwise the teacher spends her time reteaching or better yet tutoring the students left behind.

The Edutainer must be very straightforward when explaining "why" the cast operates as a whole. Each student must feel a sense of commitment.

Otherwise, this disconnected individual is the very student who prevents the success of the class from happening.

Expectations

Students' behavior is a direct reflection of what you expect and what you allow.

—The Edutainer

The classroom is in itself a small community, and any successful community establishes common goals, methods of accomplishing these goals, and how the community at large will function. Think of the entire school as being the larger body such as a city or a state. Hopefully, you, the teacher, will be provided these guidelines, and the students will be given a handbook or a written explanation of the school's policies. So we will begin with the expectations of the class.

Rules are the procedures or statements that explain what will or will not be tolerated. They should be used for the "black and white issues" of the class. Whereas expectations are a "bit more in the gray area"; these can best be explained as the mutual understandings between the parties involved.

Do you, the Edutainer, want to be directing or perhaps dictating all of the action that takes place in every scene? Or do you want to function as an entire cast that supports mutual expectations? The latter scenario would agree upon procedures for all involved and support these beliefs throughout all daily routines. The effective teacher works to instill a sense of responsibility within her students, and responsibility is earned when students are active in establishing and understanding the guidelines for their room.

Therefore the Edutainer begins her new year with a list of expectations for the entire cast, including her own role, and explaining why each is so vital for the good of the production. Students should understand and think of each as reasonable.

Rules

Rules are introduced after expectations are explained. These should be simple and always consistent as they set limits. Three to five should sufficiently cover the classroom behavior if expectations are understood first. Most important, rules have consequences that are clearly explained, must be enforced consistently, and acted upon immediately. For example, "If this infraction happens, then this is the consequence." Rules should be posted in the class, and parents should also be given a copy of your rules and an explanation of the class's expectations. We'll discuss the distribution of information in more depth in the communication chapter.

Rules can have both positive and negative consequences. For example, if an assignment is late, there are points deducted for not meeting the due date. The rationale behind this would be that half of the assignment is completing it, while the other half is getting it in on time. This rule would clearly encourage a student to "own" his work and work habits, thus teaching responsibility.

Unfortunately, this behavior elicits a negative response. Fortunately, though, it is how you, the teacher, make the student feel versus the actual consequence that the student will remember. So feelings of expectation, accountability, and respect will be some of the connotations that the student will carry with him instead of simply remembering the silent lunch or loss of recess on a particular school day.

The effective teacher means business with rules. She means what she says and only says what she means. This style of managing students is built on facts. Emotions and attitudes are not allowed. Threats are deadly, and acceptable behavior is defined through a cause-effect relationship. If "x" happens, then "y" is what follows. Good management is built from a set of expectations, which is established through rules, routines, and mutually understood behavior for the betterment of the entire class.

Consider the following consequences when rules have been violated:

- Student receives a warning
- Student is given a silent lunch or isolated during recess—either provides a time-out period, where the student is given an opportunity to think about his behavior
- Student is given morning or afternoon detention/parent is called, or written a note, to be informed of this punishment
- Conference with parents
- Conference with counselor—this depends upon the nature/severity of the issue
- Student is sent to the administration
- Student is suspended from class either using in-school or out-of-school suspension—this is usually described by individual school systems in student handbook policies (refer to Disciplinary Action Sheet in the appendix, page 181)

Handling Unwanted Behavior

Research has suggested that students do not follow rules for three different reasons. First, the student believes the teacher isn't aware of their behavior. Second, he feels that the consequence will not be given or simply overlooked. Finally, the student feels that the teacher just doesn't care. Students will always test the rules to find the limits within a class and to know if a rule will be enforced or not. And remember, when defining all of your expectations and determining the rules for the class, it is the least amount of quality that is accepted that really defines the standard of any program.

Understand that students engage in behaviors because they get something out of it, and these behaviors can produce both positive and negative effects. For example, the student who chooses to study and prepare himself for a test will more than likely do well on the assessment versus the student who chooses not to prepare himself and instead relaxes in front of the television or hangs out with friends. Although the result for each scenario is different, each student benefits either with a passing grade or simply the passing of time.

The Edutainer addresses the inappropriate behavior and not the student. First, she determines the root of the problem and understands the goal of the student. When addressing the behavior, the student needs to hear that the behavior is bad, not the person. Identify the actual words, attitude, or action—not the student. For example, telling the student not to blurt out or interrupt another student's answer is a better method of handling inappropriate behavior versus telling the student that he is being rude or acting like a know-it-all.

Second, poor behavior usually affords the student something such as attention, protection, or even simply power. The Edutainer's classroom management prevents a lot of this type of behavior. She establishes a sense of community, so students feel a sense of belonging and a feeling of being valued. How? Students are assigned daily jobs and are given responsibility with an expectation of being held accountable. An environment of wholeness is created with an "all for one and one for all attitude." Peer pressure keeps the students on their toes. Students are quick to remind one another of what each needs to do and what hasn't been done. Again, the classroom becomes a unit or somewhat of a family. The student body actually begins to take care of one another.

For example, if someone is absent, another student will do his job or get his assignments ready to be picked up by a parent. You'll be surprised that you won't even have to ask for someone to assume another's job of the week.

They really do take care of one another. Why? Because time is spent in explaining not *what* needs to be done in order for all of us to function as a class but *why* we all benefit when it does.

Finally, as power plays are concerned, the Edutainer prevents a lot of this type of behavior by presenting herself as a partner. She shows vulnerability in herself and allows the student to see her thoughts, feelings, and stances on everyday happenings as well as being able to admit she has made a mistake. Or, yikes, she might not know an immediate answer! Simply, be human. Allow the students the opportunity to see that you have a sense of humor, an ability to care, and, most important, a real desire to make a difference.

Revealing yourself as a human is easy. Tell your students stories every opportunity that you have. Begin mornings with relating how crazy getting to school can be; prove to them that you don't actually live in the classroom and that you experience the same frustrations they do when getting up and getting to school. Use humor to deal with some of the feelings of not wanting to do daily grinds—for example, always liking a particular subject, sharing a personal experience with a bad teacher you might have encountered as a student, and finding ways of being positive about coming to school for an entire day of learning.

You'll be amazed at how easy it is to create a respectful relationship with each student when you allow him to see you as a person as well as an authority figure. It is natural for students to put their best foot forward with someone with whom they share a connection. Just as you the teacher want to be acknowledged by the administration, students are motivated by the same desire. A student may question, "Why should I work so hard if no one cares?" This is not to imply that you are their friend as far as being on equal footing but instead an authority figure that they feel is friendly and has similar fears and experiences.

Positive consequences are given when rules are consistently followed. For example, if a student completes all assignments within a particular grading period, he could be rewarded with possibly having a choice of working at the different centers in the classroom or possibly given some free time for showing such responsibility and commitment to his studies. Rewards can be issued for individuals and entire classes, such as the class getting a special treat, sitting by a friend, or having ice cream on a warm afternoon.

We do not recommend assigning negative consequences for whole groups, as this is difficult to support on an individual basis. All in all, when students understand the logical relationship between their behavior and the consequence as a result of their behavior, it encourages them to cooperate and choose appropriate behavior in the future.

Moreover, students should understand the difference between what is rightfully theirs and what is earned. Learning is a student's right, whereas success is a student's choice. The good news is that once students obtain a goal or achieve success, this experience creates a desire to achieve more of that positive feeling. Therefore, the act of learning becomes one of pleasure or is an enjoyable occurrence. Bottom line—an effective teacher issues both rewards and consequences in a firm and fair way.

Reward Systems

Like it or not, reward systems do have their place in every aspect of life. You reward children with gifts for good grades, and so forth. Even as adults we like to be recognized or rewarded. These rewards could be everything from a verbal "attaboy" or a certificate of recognition to winning the Oscar in the category "Teacher of the Year." We all like the "extra" motivations we can sometimes earn. This doesn't mean students should be rewarded for everything. Rewards when used out of context—for example, as a way to get the class to be quiet—actually show a lack of management. But the Edutainer uses privileges as incentives instead of just giving them out as surprise treats.

Class Reward Systems

In the past we have used several different reward systems. It is a matter of personal choice as to what one is best. A couple of our favorites would include the bead system. This is where students are rewarded colorful beads for promptly getting settled, coming to class prepared, consistently doing well on assignments, or performing a random act of kindness to other classmates.

The teacher can decide how many and when the beads are distributed. In turn, the class has a large decorated bead jar in which to store these beads and a "Friday Bead" store for a place to shop. Being the store manager is a weekly job that is assigned, and this student also gets to select an assistant manager to help run the store. A class poster is made to post prices and encourage students to receive and save for special items.

For example, we set our shop up to include small, medium, large, and extra large prizes. Five beads are worth one dollar; we actually print class money, too. Small prizes might be worth five dollars, medium prizes ten dollars, and so on. Students are encouraged to donate gently used items, and parents purchase small one-dollar items from local retailers. Homework passes, or passes to sit by a friend or at a teacher's desk are items that are big sellers, too!

Even simple ideas such as small candy that is sold in a bag can be included as well.

One idea that works well for middle grades students is to have "Class Bucks" that they can earn. These items look like money but can have the school mascot on them. The money is earned when teachers see students being kind, helping others, talking to a new student, or doing anything that exhibits positive characteristics that you are trying to instill in the students. However, these aren't to be used as bribery for a class to behave or stay on task.

The students collect these for a period of time, such as a nine-week quarter, and then the teachers hold an auction where the students use the money to bid on items. The teachers can either purchase the items, or the parents would probably love a reason to purge their home of certain toys, games, or other items that would be suitable for the auction. Yes, this is one of those rare occasions where candy can even be used.

Other systems include:

- "Free Fridays," where a time, possibly Friday afternoon, is set aside to reward students with extra recess time, playing board games, or watching a movie for students who qualify for possibly completing all of their work, following class rules, or maintaining good grades.
- "Group or table rewards," where stars, stickers, or pen checks are put on a chart each time a set of students get started, complete work, or simply transition well from one activity to the next. The idea here is that each student encourages the other to do well. When an agreed upon number is achieved, this group of students receives ice cream, or possibly an opportunity to sit with another class at lunch, or maybe a free pass for homework or even an opportunity to spend extra time in the computer lab. Rewards can be weekly or even monthly.
- Ticket, clothespin (token economy). Each Monday a student is given a certain number of tickets or clothespins. Any time a student breaks a rule or displays unacceptable behavior then he must pay with one of these items. At the end of the week, the remaining tickets or pins are turned into points to eventually use for items in a treasure box such as candy, free time, decorative pencils or erasers, stickers, etc.
- Draw your name from a hat/bucket. The idea here is that if a student has successfully accomplished good grades, good behavior, completing all work in a timely manner, or any other agreed upon goal, his

name is put into a bucket, and the student has the opportunity to receive some type of prize. This could include a pass to a chosen activity—for example, free time, extra art or music time, or possibly being the teacher's helper. Drawings are usually completed at the end of the week. Students may know what the drawing is for or it could be a surprise that the teacher shares after the name is drawn from the bucket.

Individual Rewards

Individual rewards can range from simple rewards such as allowing a student to write with colored pens or markers to something more elaborate such as having lunch with a special friend, teacher, or even the principal. Individual rewards may also be extra motivation for students to work on assignments that require more time and effort such as science fair projects. These projects are usually required even though most of the work is done outside of school. Students may feel this is just too much work for just a grade and a project that will be thrown away after the science fair.

However, if you were to offer a reward for the students who win a ribbon then they may be more motivated to work on the projects. Based upon school or district policies, you may, with parent permission, be able to take the students to Pizza Hut for lunch. At the very least you should be able to buy them lunch and let them have a little party in your classroom or somewhere on campus.

Other rewards may include:

- Draw on the wipe board or classroom board
- Complete only half or receive a free homework pass
- Move your desk next to a friend or in front of the class as the teacher
- Teach with the teacher
- Sit in a special chair or on the floor
- Be a helper for a younger class
- Share a special book or something brought from home
- Keep something special on your desk—maybe a stuffed animal or picture from home
- Listen to music during a selected time of the day
- Be the leader for the day or for a special game
- Free rental coupons for Blockbuster
- Coupons for movie theater

Routines

Management is nothing more than motivating other people.

—Lee Iacocca

Any effective classroom is built upon a predictable set of routines. These habits offer the students a sense of security and a feeling of familiarity while they are training to perform a variety of activities. Though the old saying "familiarity breeds contempt" may be true in some instances, students are more likely to be successful when they know what the teacher expects and what is expected of them. An unknown or unfamiliar environment proves just the opposite. Just as establishing class expectations and rules took a good bit of time, teaching routines, learning chores, and developing good work habits are crucial.

Again, research has shown that effective teachers who maintain classroom management invest a great deal of time in the beginning of the year; others, who are too quick to get into the textbooks, spend the rest of the year wishing they had. Think about how much time is wasted every day in each classroom with transitioning, repeating expectations, and simply waiting for the students' attention only to explain something one more time.

By and large, elementary teachers will spend most of their time doing this, but junior high students still need these lessons. By the time the student gets to high school, he is given minimal direction explaining the "1, 2, 3s" of classroom behavior. Simply put, model and explain what behavior is expected. The end result is that practice makes perfect. The act of teaching becomes front and center because distractions and interruptions are minimized.

Managing the Students

If our students are so gifted, why do we treat them like idiots? Furthermore, why do we do for our children what they are capable of doing for themselves? This in itself robs them of any kind of responsibility and a sense of belonging to the community not to mention a personal sense of satisfaction.

Personal Responsibility

The effective teacher assigns the classroom jobs and rotates them weekly. The classroom is a community and therefore requires everyone to pitch in and help. These responsibilities can be done in the morning, throughout the day, or as needed just as long as they are completed on a regular daily basis. Again, think routine.

When these jobs are assigned, the effective teacher explains not only where everything is located in the classroom but also how it is used and why.

Students learn through hearing, seeing, and doing. And this takes time. Presenting and practicing expectations of behaviors are not accomplished in one day or even the first week of school. They are presented, explained, and continually rehearsed.

Personal Accountability

We've all been in the classroom where, once the teacher is finished explaining the lesson and the students are assigned some independent work, the helpless learner takes center stage, whether it be a raised hand in the air or a swift leap to the teacher's desk. This syndrome can quickly be identified; sometimes the student simply wants the teacher to read the written directions aloud and follows with a quick "Oh, I get it." Other times there is a case of real confusion, and the teacher is left reteaching or individually tutoring the student. How can this scenario be prevented?

First, the Edutainer must evaluate her teaching methods. Did she say it, explain it, demonstrate it, and practice it? If so, the lesson has been thoroughly taught.

Begin a lesson and complete it. Don't start then stop with one idea only to jump to another. If you're having trouble staying on one topic, imagine what your student is experiencing. All types of learners are able to grasp a concept when they hear it, see it, and have a chance to personally practice it. This is not to say that there won't be any questions with a well-taught lesson, but this practice will alleviate a lot of the "I don't understand what we're suppose to do" plague.

Second, the Edutainer provides clear and thorough directions to the assignment. This would include stating/reading directions, providing examples, and even modeling an answer or two. The Edutainer then allows an opportunity for students to ask questions or get clarification.

Third, the Edutainer must expect that all of her students are capable of helping themselves. Allow students the opportunity to help themselves before helping them. Again, helping and taking the responsibility of the assignment are two different behaviors.

Managing the Daily Schedule

Now that the physical part of the classroom has been explained, the effective teacher also needs to think about the flow of the school day.

- Transitions need to be made smoothly, and the manner in which students are expected to use the classroom requires explanation. Let students know in advance that a lesson or activity will be ending.

Consider giving students a "two-minute warning" when one activity is going to end and another begin.

- What are students to do when they have finished assigned work? Remember, every student works at his own pace, so there will be staggered completion times for assignments. What is your plan for utilizing this instructional time that is productive and an opportunity for chatter chaos?

- Determine times that students are to turn work in for the day. Is all work to be put in correctly labeled bins in the morning or is work called for throughout the day when the class begins? There is no right or wrong answer here. This can only be determined how you, the Edutainer, can best manage the paper load. We also like the idea of assigning a job for checking papers. Here, a student is given the task of using a clipboard and checking off names and numbers of papers that are simply turned into the bin. As the teacher, you'll immediately know the difference between a missing assignment and a late assignment.

- Consider how you are going to keep up with missing versus absent work in a grade book. We like the idea of drawing a box around an absent student's missing grade and underscoring a late assignment. You just need to be able to make a distinction between the two.

- What is your plan for work without a name? Use a large clip—possibly a magnetic one that will hold to the front board. Label it "Lost and Found." Students who are checked for missing assignments can claim their work here.

- Determine a late work policy for you and your grade level. If an assignment is a day late, how many points will be deducted? The higher the grade level, the more points should be removed. For example, a fifth grader should have a more rigorous penalty than a third grader. The scale should be aligned within your immediate grade level as well as those above and below you.

- Use a homework notice that requires a parent signature. This allows the parent to immediately become aware of weak or unorganized study skills and "flags" the work as late the following day.

- Remember mass mutiny is just minutes away! Therefore, effective teachers are proactive rather than reactive. Remember, your new batch of students does not know you, and Mrs. "So and So" from last year might have let them get away with anything. Don't risk or ASSUME that just because these small people are occupying space in your room, they understand how to behave under your guidance. Teach them.

- Mold them by modeling and explaining each routine in a firm and patient manner. When the student practices the desired behavior, recognize it. Just as when the student's behavior does not comply with class expectations, take the time to redirect or address it. This teacher interaction speaks volumes as to what will be tolerated or rejected.
- You dismiss students—not a bell or other students changing classes in the hall. But be sure to stick to the schedule. The bell-to-bell schedule has to work for all of the classes involved.
- Be clear as to what you expect to happen when students enter or exit the classroom: "Come in and record today's assignments" or "Before leaving, make sure all papers are picked up and chairs are pushed under the desks." Students are not born knowing to do this.
- Are students to line up in front of the door? To the side of the door? Wait to be told when to enter the room? What is the traffic pattern if the students exchange classrooms during the day?
- What is your policy for forgetting a book or personal item in another class? Are students allowed to return to the previous class or homeroom once a lesson has begun? However, if you decide against the student returning for his forgotten book, how will he function without it? Have a plan either way.

One of the best strategies for thinking about all the daily routines your students will encounter is to visualize each day. How do they enter the room? Do they know where to sit? When do they sharpen their pencils? What if they need to get a dictionary? None of these routines can be taken for granted if all of the members of the class are expected to function in a specific manner. It is up to you, the Edutainer, to run the show and that means without chaos and interruptions.

It is impossible to predict every possible occurrence for each individual teacher. Instead the effective teacher and her students will organize routines and consistently perform each while making minor modifications as they move throughout the year. Remember to acclaim students for modeling correct behavior, too. Here is a list of procedures that you might want to practice with your students:

- Entering the classroom
- Morning work
- Using the student supply center
- Keeping work areas organized

- Asking for help
- Passing/exchanging /collecting papers
- Returning assignments (make-up and late work, too)
- Moving about the room
- Listening to announcements
- Preparing for emergencies: fires, tornadoes, evacuation, etc.
- When you are absent
- Using the student agenda
- Forgetting supplies in locker
- Lining up
- Recess/lunchroom behavior
- Using hall and bathroom passes

Multi-Management

Rather than use the term multitasking, which denotes you doing all the work, we use the term multi-management, which means that you are similar to a producer/director that manages many aspects of the daily performance. This includes the other cast members such as the students, assistants, and parents, and managing administrative (noninstructional) tasks, such as taking attendance, collecting money and forms, planning field trips, and other aspects of managing the entire "production."

We suggest making a list of these items and determining whether this is something a student, assistant, or even parent could be assigned. Don't fall into the day and hope that you will remember to do all of these extra duties with the responsibility of teaching lessons and managing students. Intentions are great but methods are much better. Have a plan instead of a hope of getting it all done (refer to Edutainer Professional Agenda in the appendix, page 183).

Remember the jobs from the organization chapter that we discussed? These are rotated weekly. Try to delegate a few of these duties here. If not, how about other willing parties? Obviously, if you are in the lower elementary school, these tasks could not be assumed by a five-year-old. However, systems could be put in place that would make doing some of these jobs a bit less time consuming. For example, if students are asked to unstack their chairs in the morning and have a seat in an assigned desk/table, attendance could be done with a quick glance of seeing what chairs are not returned to the desk from the previous afternoon. Note to self: do not ask the five-year-old to sharpen the scissors.

DID YOU KNOW . . . Children actually need consistent rules to feel safe. Children thrive in ordered environments.

Moreover, if homeroom lists are made with students' names and corresponding columns, quick checks could be used to denote which students have returned requested items. Our point is, the Edutainer is always thinking ahead of the immediate moment. What thought or action could prevent a simple task of collecting items from being handled twice? Generic spreadsheets or even simple lined paper with homeroom or class names can easily eliminate collecting wads of paper to be thrown onto your desk in the morning only to have to sort through the pile a second time to determine what has been returned. Handle a task one time and cover it thoroughly.

Parents make wonderful resources when it comes to handling class parties, monthly birthday celebrations, or decorating bulletin boards (refer to Volunteers Needed Handout in the appendix, page 184). With minimal instruction and good communication, noninstructional activities can easily be delegated to willing and able volunteers. Remember, exactly who is running this production?!

Stress Management

One aspect of management that is often overlooked is stress management. However, if an Edutainer is to be consistently on stage performing, she has to handle stress. Remember, "teacher burnout" is a very real problem, especially with new teachers. While the purpose of the entire book is to develop the "core" skills needed to prepare and perform effectively as an Edutainer, they will not eliminate all the stress. So, here are some tips to help you deal with the stress.

- An apple a day. Okay, maybe you don't have to eat an apple everyday, but focus on eating healthier. You are a product of the food you eat.
- Be proactive in your preparation. Reactive people have higher stress.
- Spend some time rebonding with your class, especially about halfway through the year.
- Leave your teaching at school.
- Get plenty of sleep.
- Start an exercise routine you will stick with. Remember, twenty-one days to form a new habit.

- Laughter is the best medicine. Laugh daily!
- Play relaxing music in the classroom.
- Ask for help when needed.
- Read this book twice a year!

Top Edutainer Tips for Successful Classroom Management

- Have a plan—heck, overplan! Extra time can be a teacher's worst nightmare. See our intermission ideas that can turn unexpected time into enlightening time.
- Communicate positively—your students and parents must know your expectations and procedures. Everyone needs to be on the same page. There is no such thing as overcommunicating, just overlooking.
- Connect with students in a personal way; let them know that you believe in them.
- Be clear; be fair; be approachable—this includes students and parents. Remember, you can't fix what you don't know about.
- Don't put off until tomorrow what can be done today. The effective teacher has a plan for handling papers, lists, and people. Methods and strategies are put into place, so that tasks are handled once.
- Be proactive, not reactive—being put on the defense brings out everyone's emotions; unfortunately, usually not the best.
- Be the person you expect others to be; model your best.
- Have fun—if you're not enjoying being in the classroom, chances are others aren't enjoying it either.

INTERMISSION 2

Activities and Games

If there is one area where the Edutainer can really shine, it is when she shares some fun or interesting activities. The Edutainer's intermission is built around "thinking activities" that can be included in daily lesson planning or can be implemented as "sponge activities." These can be used during a few idle minutes left in a class or when a lesson is interrupted by an unplanned event. Like any good performer, it is always important to have a bag of ideas that can "entertain" or engage the audience in any given setting.

Games

Compound Chain Game
This activity is designed to build students' vocabulary by focusing on compounds words. To start the game, have a preset order in which the students will take turns. You will also need a timer, or you can estimate a reasonable amount of time in which the students need to answer. The teacher starts the game by saying a compound word such as "hotdog." Then the first student has to say a compound word using either "hot" or "dog," such as "corndog," or "hotshot."

If the student is unable to answer in the specified time limit, he gets "gonged" and is out of the game. If he answers correctly, such as "corndog," then the next student has to say a compound word using either "corn" or "dog," such as "popcorn." The game continues until there is one person remaining.

Word Play

This game is used to help develop the students' vocabulary as well. Each student has a white board and marker, or even notebook paper will do. The teacher chooses a word such as "said." Then she asks the students to write another word based upon the part of speech she shares. For example, if the teacher asks for the adjective part of speech for "speak" the students would write, "speaking." If the teacher asks for a vivid verb, then the students would write the word "exclaimed." You can have students match up head to head and move to the next round, or you can have teams where points are given for each correct answer.

Bread or Toast

This activity can be used for extra credit, a reward, or just a fun break at the end of a class. It is designed to improve critical thinking, problem solving, or reasoning skills. This can include premade worksheets or questions that you have on an overhead or the board. These types of questions would include word problems, analogies, unscrambling words (such as science vocabulary), or word spellings (such as blends and vowel and consonant patterns).

The students have a time limit within which to complete the work. When they turn the assignment in, if it is all correct, the work is put in the "bread basket," and if there is any mistake the work is "burned toast" and put in the wastebasket. The teacher can select a winner or several winners to award extra points, homework passes, or just plain "kudos to you."

Trash Basketball

This activity is one of those games that is used as a review before an exam. First the teacher randomly chooses a score keeper (using a number between one and one hundred that the students have written down). Then the teacher divides the students into two teams. Questions are asked alternately to members of each team. The teacher asks the questions in order by going down rows of each team. If the student answers the question correctly, he has the choice of taking one point, or he can risk that point and shoot a waffle ball into the trashcan for three points. If the student misses the shot, then no point is given.

However, if the student misses the question, then anyone on the other team can raise his hand to answer the question. The teacher only gives the other team one chance to answer the question, so the team must be certain of the answer. If someone on the other team "steals" a question, then he has the choice of taking a point or shooting for three points as well. The winning team (and score keeper) gets five points extra credit on their exams.

Note: This is a crowd favorite. Some students will study for the trash bas-ketball review game that would not normally study for an exam because they will get to "shoot" if they correctly answer the questions.

Jamaica Trip (Name Game)

This is an activity that can be used on the first day of school to help the teacher and other students to learn everyone's names. This game is great because it starts to build a connection with the teacher and students. This activity is a word association game where students choose something that be-gins with the first letter of their first name. For instance, if a student's name were Josh, he would choose a word like "Jolly-Rancher." The game is played as if the class is going on a trip to Jamaica and everyone is taking something with them. The goal is to remember what everyone's name is and what item each person is taking with him on the trip.

The game begins with the teacher coming up with a word for her first name as well. So let's say the teacher's name is Gloria. Then she would come up with a word like "gloves." Then the teacher says, "My name is Gloria; I am going to Jamaica, and I am taking gloves." Then the students go in order adding each person in front of them. For instance, if the first student after the teacher were Josh, he would say, "My name is Josh; I am going to Jamaica with Gloria and her gloves, and I am taking some Jolly-Ranchers." The game progresses until each student has taken a turn, and the game finishes with the teacher. Here, she names every student and what each is taking on the trip.

Note: Don't let students write down anything during the activity. Some are afraid they won't remember, but since it is word association, students usually do better than they expect to do.

The name game is really a great way to begin developing relationships with students. Besides learning their names, you may find out a little about them by the word they choose and since you let them use your first name (for the game only) it gives them a glimpse into you as a person rather than just a teacher. One student, named Taylor, who used the word "tortellini" in the name game, actually brought in tortellini soup mix and beautiful bowls as a Christmas present. So you can see how something as simple as this game can begin to build relationships with your students.

Dictionary Debate

This is another game that helps students develop vocabulary and word skills.

Each student has a white board and marker, or notebook paper will do. They are divided into two teams. The teacher chooses a word such as "jump."

She will then ask for a synonym or an antonym. Each team is given a point for each correct answer. However, if an answer is duplicated within a team then the answer is thrown out, and no point is given. For instance, if the teacher asks for a synonym for the word "jump" and more than one person on the same team answers "leap," then no point is awarded. This rule helps stretch the vocabulary of the students and also helps alleviate any desire to look at a teammate's answer on his white board.

Lawyer at Large

This is an activity that can be used in any given subject area. A teacher chooses a topic, such as the Revolutionary War. The teacher then makes an opinionated statement, such as "The colonies should have been defeated by the Redcoats." The students then have to prove the statement based upon the facts given in the texts, book, stories, and so forth. An extra twist that can be used is to have some students defend the statement and have another group of students try to prove the statement wrong.

As long as students can support their position with facts, their answer is valid. This is also a great exercise when teaching novels. Students can learn that a general idea or opinion can be correct as long as it is validated in factual content from a given short story, novel, or even a poem. Students learn to think for themselves and to use the text as a tool to validate their thinking.

"Teacher Says," Otherwise Known as "Simon Says"

This activity is an adaptation of the old Simon Says game. The game begins slowly, so the students think the exercise will be easy. Then the teacher increases the difficulty. Each student has a white board and marker, or, again, notebook paper will do. We will use math for this example. The teacher picks a number and says "the teacher says four." So the students all write down the number four, either the numeral or the word.

Then the teacher could say, "Teacher says 320," so students write 320. The teacher can further increase the difficulty by saying, "teacher says three million, four hundred thousand, six hundred twelve and six tenths." The students need to write 3,400,612.6 to be correct. Place value, fractions, percents, and decimals are great for this activity.

Obviously, teacher discretion is used when playing this game and working with either a remedial, average, or enriched group of students. The wonderful aspect of this exercise is that it can really be used to reach all levels of learners.

Jeopardy

This is an adaptation of the television show. You can make up a board with categories and value level or you can find computer-generated boards on the Internet, some that are already set up by subject areas. You can also find links to Jeopardy PowerPoints on our website. Other similar games would include Concentration and 25,000 Pyramid.

Create Your Own

Think of pop culture hits such as *American Idol* or *America's Got Talent* to include in your lessons by modifying them to fit with the material. For example, let students come up with a dance for the circulatory system, or make a commercial that includes concepts from social studies class.

ACT III

THE PERFORMANCE

SCENE 6

Communication

I remind myself every morning: Nothing I say this day will teach me anything.
So if I'm going to learn, I must do it by listening.

—Larry King

One of the most effective skills of an Edutainer is the ability to communicate. This includes listening as well as speaking. The communication of ideas and concepts is important for an Edutainer to relate to her target audience and cast. The cast consists of the four Ps: parents, pupils, principal (administration), and partners (faculty and staff). If the Edutainer can learn to communicate effectively with all cast members, then misunderstandings or misconceptions can easily be addressed or alleviated. Therefore it will be the goal of this chapter to help you polish your means and methods of communicating, so your delivery is worthy of a standing ovation.

The Cast of Performers

First let's identify the cast that we are working with, so we can understand their needs and role in the communication process. The four Ps become a strong supporting cast that is focused; and when everyone is on the same team, your ultimate outcome, student success, is more likely to be *achieved*.

Edmund's teacher said, " Two negatives can form a positive, but two positives can never form a negative."

Figure 6.1.

Principal

Communication with your administration can greatly influence your work environment. If the principal is an effective administrator then communication can be beneficial to both of you. Competent administrators welcome dialogue with the effective teacher and are there to support her in the classroom. When having to call upon the principal, consider these thoughts:

- Have I done everything in my power to handle the student and/or parent?
- Do I have clear and factual documentation to show my involvement and steps that have been taken?
- Before complaining or making cases against a policy or situation, do I have some suggestions to improve the current one?
- Have I expressed an interest to take an active role in being a supportive staff member?

Parent

There are no second chances when it comes to connecting with parents. You have been entrusted with their most prized possession, and whatever you say about their children, you are saying about them. We have found that the more you involve parents in your classroom, the more supportive they become of you and your classroom. We realize that it is easier to involve parents in the elementary level than in the secondary schools, but it is to your advantage to keep them feeling connected and aware of what is happening with their child's classroom regardless of their grade.

Pupil

We often forget that children are people, too. They have fears, dreams, insecurities, and issues just like adults do. Sometimes it's easy to minimize their feelings because, well, they are just kids. However, as an Edutainer, if you can empathize and relate to the students through their personal experiences and yours, then you can make connections from a learning perspective as well. As an effective teacher it is up to you to motivate the student to be accountable and show them how to make learning a meaningful experience. Good effective communicators address the following in any given lesson.

- What is this? Introduce a new idea with something that is familiar to them. Analogies are great here or use "What if" stories to connect the lesson to the student.
- Why do I need to know this? Explain a purpose for the content.
- What do you want me to do with this? Use clear step-by-step explanations throughout the lesson.
- How do I know that I am finished and/or that I actually get it? Use either informal or formal types of assessment to determine whether the lesson's objective was achieved or not understood.

Partners

Remember that your colleagues are enduring the same stress as you are. Keep in mind that you are all part of the same production, whether the scene is a team meeting, group conference, or faculty meeting. This does not mean that you will agree on everything, so learn to "major on the majors" and "minor on the minors." There will be times when you simply have to "agree to disagree," with respect for another's opinion. It helps to remember that each teacher brings something good to the table and that we all have our own unique gifts to share. Bottom line—always treat other teachers professionally and with respect.

Remember the entire staff, too. This includes the janitor, cafeteria worker, secretary, and assistants, who are all part of the daily performance. During one of our block experiences as an education major, a mentoring teacher had shared some personal advice. One of the first things he told us was that the staff were the most important people to a teacher.

This particular teacher would bring donuts to the janitors and cafeteria workers. He would always say hello and take time to have dialogue with them. This teacher never worried if he needed something cleaned or fixed in his classroom. Not to mention he usually received a more than generous amount of food at lunch or that last piece of pie in the cafeteria. Not that we necessarily need or even want a larger serving of food, but you can see how respect can be reciprocal and beneficial to all the cast in the performance. The Edutainer knows that ALL the players in the performance play a significant role. Everyone wants to feel appreciated.

Communication Skills

Communication skills are most important when we talk about winning the hearts of our listeners. The tone, volume, rhythm, and body language of the communicator play a vital role when speaking both directly and indirectly.

Tone
Tone is the expression of a mood or emotion. When speaking, your tone should be pleasant, friendly, and inviting. When expressing assurance, your tone needs to lower at the end of your sentence. If your voice becomes higher, it can convey that you are unsure or even questioning your own statements. Finally, make sure you have good posture when speaking. Present yourself as the confident leader that others can rely on and trust.

Rhythm
Be aware of your pace when speaking. If you talk too slowly, then you risk losing the interest of your audience. However, if you speak too quickly, your listeners may become confused or may not understand what you are saying. When you have a key point to make, make it, and then be quiet for a moment. Silence can actually be an effective part of speaking. As with tone, make sure there is inflection and change in the rhythm of your speech. Remember, if you are nervous, you could have a tendency to speak too quickly, so relax, take a deep breath, and captivate your audience.

Volume
Your speaking volume depends upon the size of your audience and the vastness of the room. If you are talking in a large area, then you'll need to project your voice, so everyone in the audience can hear you. There is nothing more frustrating than listening to a presentation on a topic of interest when you

can't hear the speaker. Don't forget to emphasize key words or phrases for effect, too. If you talk too softly, you can appear anxious or afraid. Speak with authority yet with humility. Allow the audience to hear your knowledge and perceive your authenticity.

Body Language

Believe it or not, we communicate more through our body language than our actual words. In fact, if there is a disparity between your body language and words, people will believe your actions, over your words. Have you ever had a conversation with someone where you could tell they were trying too hard to be nice and their body language was shouting that they wish you would simply go away? Keep this in mind when speaking to the students, parents, or any audience. When you are speaking, look directly into the eyes of your listeners. Eye contact shows respect and interest.

Again, posture is also important to body language, so stand or sit up straight. Relax your shoulders; upper body tightness reflects tension or nervousness. You might want to consider moving among the audience as you speak. However, don't pace back and forth, as this can be distracting to your listeners or represent anxiety. Practice being relaxed, comfortable, and as natural as possible. Ultimately, effective communication is about connecting with the audience.

"The Art of Connecting" with Students

The secret in education lies in respecting the student.

—Ralph Waldo Emerson

The "art of connecting" is the ability to form a significant bond between the speaker and listener. This connection determines how valuable the shared information becomes to the listener. Therefore, the greater the relationship, the more meaningful the information becomes. It is almost a separate curriculum all within itself. In laymen's terms it is not so much

---

DID YOU KNOW . . . Communication is:

7 percent what you say (words)

38 percent how you say it (volume, pitch, rhythm, etc.)

55 percent your body language (facial expressions, posture, etc.)

Source: A. Barbour (2000).

"what the speaker is saying" but rather "to what extent" the information is being understood.

In the classroom setting, connecting skills lead to creative and effective approaches to solving problems and getting work accomplished. These skills create the climate of the classroom as well as develop the students' self-esteem. According to Sylvia Habel, president of William Glasser Institute of Australia, "The teachers that inspired me were the ones that related to me; it was as though they were talking to the 'me' inside as though they knew me somehow."

Respect

The effective teacher's communication must convey empathy, which is the ability to communicate care and concern, to her students. While doing so, she cultivates a respectful environment. Her students feel they can trust her without fear of embarrassment, lack of acceptance, or receiving preconceived judgment. Hands are willingly raised, risks are taken when students aren't confident of their knowledge or individual answer, and an authentic kindness is witnessed with both parties—teacher and student alike.

The Edutainer treats her students just the way she wishes to be cared for in the classroom. This behavior is modeled through attentive eye contact, listening, and expressing a genuine interest when another is speaking. According to Kathy Cox, Georgia's state superintendent, "Nothing is more important to the student's success than a positive relationship with the teacher regardless of interferences to their education such as a tough home life, limited parental support or socioeconomic level."

Positive Motivation

Good motivation produces good learning outcomes. Many students simply don't understand why they need to study curriculum that doesn't seem relevant to them. The Edutainer introduces and explains the significance of that material. She makes personal connections to the real world that the student isn't able to do for himself. As a result, the students get motivated and act upon their interest while studying that subject. The Edutainer can share stories having to do with the lesson's key idea. Students are more apt to remember an idea if they can personalize it by attaching a memory or possibly a personal meaning to it.

The Edutainer might also have the students make personal reflections with the lesson's objectives. This suggestion often helps the students to stop and think about what is being said. It's another way of asking your listeners to paraphrase what they think you have said. This strategy is a win-win situation, as it keeps the students engaged in the lesson and also requires "active" listening skills.

Feedback

The effective teacher provides immediate feedback when possible—for example, during class discussions. The teacher would not wait for the end of the class to provide feedback from a student's comments made earlier during a discussion. Of course, some feedback cannot be instantaneous—for example, homework, tests, or quizzes. This can be a challenge, as described by Kathy Cox: "We have an instant result's mentality; we have no patience for learning, results, or growth. The focus is always on instant feedback." However, the longer the wait time from when the work was completed to the student receiving comments, the less meaningful the feedback becomes.

Verbal

In verbal feedback, the teacher speaks to a student, either privately or publicly, to provide behavior or task-specific information about the student's academic or behavioral performance. Positive comments about "on target" answers in class discussions go a long way with students' self-esteem. "Awesome" or "Right on the money" are quick feedback opportunities to keep students in the arena of learning. Sharing grade point averages or exceptional grades on projects, tests, or quizzes are also great ways to keep the students motivated with their learning.

Nonverbal

Nonverbal feedback is feedback that the teacher provides to a student with his or her actions. Examples of nonverbal feedback include smiling, patting a student's shoulder, and making eye contact. Nonverbal feedback is important in establishing and maintaining a rapport with a student, and teachers should be conscious of their actions in this regard. The "teacher look" can be very effective here. Examples of this would include the "raised eyebrow," a long pause when speaking, or simply shaking your head; often these can be more powerful than directly speaking to a student.

Physical proximity can also help redirect students' attention or behavior. It is a good idea to move about the room while directly teaching or observing students on task. Touch your students' shoulders, desks, or even books/papers.

You would be amazed at how this simple gesture shows them that you care. The ability of a teacher to use silence is usually effective, too. Like the pregnant pause, silence can build anticipation.

Written

Written feedback is similar, except that this type of feedback provides a more black and white record of the teacher's comments. Written feedback may be given on an assignment in a casual comment or number or appear in the form of a report card. All valuable responses including written feedback should be specific, accurate, and stress the positives whenever possible. Even the most blunt or forthright comments should always leave the student with dignity.

> There are times when silence has the loudest voice.
>
> —Leroy Brownlow

Understanding

The effective teacher seeks to understand and be understood. Most students don't like being told what to do. They often want a chance to have a say in what goes on in the classroom and a chance to prove it will work. In solving classroom problems, it is better to listen first before jumping in to direct. Class rules can be formed to figure out solutions to problems, and the effective teacher empowers her students to carry out the solutions. Students who can identify what needs to be done are more likely to take on greater responsibility for getting the task accomplished.

Therefore the effective teacher seeks to understand the problem from the "point of view" of the problem solvers, that is, her students, rather than force her idea as to how the problem needs to be handled. This approach to problem solving helps to improve interpersonal skills between the teacher and her students. Sylvia Habel notes, "I believe both student and teacher need to learn about their internal motivations and how to read and understand others' behavior. Learning how to express one's needs, how to get what they want in a responsible and effective way and how to give useful feedback can begin being taught at a very young age." Often, sharing a relevant story of your own experiences in similar situations can prove helpful in opening meaningful dialogue. This openness reveals both humanity and vulnerability of the teacher.

DID YOU KNOW . . . The word *silent* contains the exact same letters as the word *listen*.

Edutainer Tips for Communicating:

- Do not substitute technology for communication.
- Communicate professionally—avoid emotional negative responses.
- Be sensitive to misinterpretation, whether verbal or written.
- Never underestimate the importance of effective communication.
- Keep doors of communication open.
- Remember, listening is important element of communication.

Establishing Parent Communication

It is an amazing partnership when the parents and the teacher are together for the sake of the student's success.

—Lily Eskelsen

Once the room is prepared and the students are welcomed, the parents need to be contacted. The Edutainer understands the importance of this relationship. Getting parents positively involved in her classroom should be initiated during the first two weeks of school. Let's begin with some basic introductions:

- Make phone calls during the first week of school to welcome both the student and parent to your class. Introduce yourself and explain that information will be sent home to explain the basics of the class. Be sure to refer them to a possible class web page and remind them of the scheduled open house or curriculum night.
- If open house is a few weeks away, prepare some general information and list opportunities for parents to get involved in the class. Send this information home by the end of the first week. Be sure to include your school e-mail address as well as a request that the parent(s) send you an e-mail. This allows you the opportunity to have their current e-mail address. All too many times cell numbers and e-mail addresses change over the summer. This is a great way to eliminate having to search for an updated one later in the year.
- Ideas for class web page:
  - Information on upcoming lessons, units, or chapters
  - Explanation of rules, expectations, and class policies
  - Updates of future tests, projects, or class events
  - Information, such as a "homework hotline"
  - Tips for parents' and students' success both in and outside the classroom

- Compose a friendly letter or creative pamphlet/brochure to your students and parents during the first week of school. Introduce yourself personally and professionally. Include family, personal interests, experience, and expectations. This is a great way of allowing both student and parent to understand how you operate and what you expect for the upcoming year. Remember to keep it friendly and positive! (See "Friendly Letter" in the appendix, page 187.)

- Create and send home the student questionnaire (see Student Survey Form in the appendix, page 166). This idea allows the parent to describe your new student from their perspective. This paper includes areas of strengths, weaknesses, personal interests, and any information that the parent feels is important for you as the teacher to know.

- Depending on your school policy, most elementary classes use a weekly or biweekly folder to correspond with the parents. It is sent home on a Thursday or Friday afternoon and returned the following Monday. This folder has two pockets. One is labeled "For Your Information" or "Items to Keep." The other pocket might be labeled "Please Review, Sign, and Return." This side of the folder includes graded work that is stapled with a cover letter. This letter includes the student's name and weekly date, and requires a parent signature.

- We also like to include "weekly updates" or "upcoming events." Here is a quick opportunity to remind parents of upcoming field trips or maybe items that the students will need for special projects. This folder serves two purposes. The first is the opportunity for the parent to see the student's work. The second is the opportunity to send/receive any information, money, or signatures. Enforce this routine with both the student and parent. Incentives are great here. For example, if the whole class returns its "Friday Folders" for the first month, the class might be entitled to an ice cream or movie treat.

Open House: Your First Debut

Just like any other time you invite guests to join you, the scenery looks neat and clean and as the leading role, you are prepared and looking your best. Open house is an opportunity for the parents to see the classroom, the curriculum, and you. They want to see how you act. Are you organized, friendly, intelligent? Most important, are you capable of teaching and taking care of their child? The answer is yes, and now is the time for you to shine!

Begin to think about open house weeks before, so you can gather your thoughts about what you would like to share and have samples of work that would represent what is being discussed. Consider having your students write

> DID YOU KNOW . . . Most problems between teachers and parents are a result of miscommunication or simply a lack of communication.

an invitation to send home to the parents. Remember, some might need two if they come from a divorced family setting. Think about how you would like to display the students' work. Create a tangible handout of the evening's main ideas, create sign-up opportunities for parents to get involved, and consider posting conference times if needed (see Open House example in the appendix, pages 188–90, for samples of these).

Suggestions for a "Five-Star Evening"

- Be sure all students' names are on the desks and that cubbies/hooks for their belongings are labeled.
- Tidy all equipment, resources, and inside area of desks.
- Share a sample of all students' work on a selected wall/bulletin board or at individual students' desks.
- Arrange the room that is most accommodating for a "sold out" show and its busy traffic pattern. Remember, these adults sitting in the chairs are not your typical sized students.
- Prepare front boards with any reminders about information that the parents need to pick up, sign up, or simply fill out while waiting for all guests to arrive. Have a sharpened pencil at each desk with a handout reviewing the evening's ideas; this is something a parent can preview while waiting for the evening to begin.
- Think about having the students write a "Dear Mom or Dad" letter welcoming her or him to the class. This can be put on top of the student's desk. Another fun idea is to supply the parents with an index card and a sharpened pencil at each desk, so they can write back to their child. Suggestions might be words of encouragement for a successful year or simple comments about how nice the student keeps his or her desk.
- Consider having one or two name labels on each student's desk for parents to fill out and wear during the open house. This way you will be able to address them by name when speaking to them.
- Be prepared for the evening—jot down notes for yourself along with a copy of the parent handout. Rehearse the order and ideas before actually presenting.
- Gather and display a copy of all students' texts and workbooks, so the parents can see what book is used for what lesson/class.

- Try to meet/greet each parent who enters the room; make them feel welcome and if possible say something about his or her child.
- Introduce yourself and share about your immediate family, personal interests, professional experience, and a brief philosophy of how you feel about education.
- Share class expectations and rules.
- Briefly review curriculum.
- Discuss daily schedules, routines, and materials that are needed.
- Mention lunch and snack times—suggestions or restrictions.
- Explain absent/late work policies.
- Discuss student responsibilities with writing down assignments.
- Discuss homework expectations—how much and how often it will be given.
- Discuss methods of parent/teacher communication—for example, e-mail addresses for you and parents, best times to reach you by phone and at what number, and weekly folder system.
- Discuss grading policy, progress reports, and final report card times.
- Allow time for question/answer time—request all be pertinent to the group and save individual concerns for conferences or a brief time following the open house.
- Thank all for attending and remind them that you are a team that will work best together both at home and at school to support their child's success.
- Remember to smile; let the parents know that you are excited to be their child's teacher and have your students best interests at heart . . . breathe.

Maintaining Parent Communication

One of the most common complaints among parents is that had they known that their child was assigned the work, they could have helped the student with his or her responsibilities. Given this grievance, the Edutainer chooses to be proactive. Therefore an effective teacher communicates not once but several times with her students and families when assigning work and due dates. Both children and adults need constant reminders.

Think about when you make appointments with a dentist or hair salon. Doesn't each of these offices call and remind you to confirm the appointment that they have set aside a time to provide you with a service? And, believe it or not, even when we have made the appointment ourselves, written it down in a day planner of some type, and received a follow-up call, haven't we still missed an appointment or two?

Keeping that in mind, do we really believe that when we tell our students who are maybe seven or thirteen that they are going to be given a test or a project that they are going to remember it? Therefore, we believe that students and parents need to see something, hear that something, and then write that something down—not once or twice, but three times. Yes, three times is a charm.

For the first time, have the students write down daily all upcoming assignments in a daily agenda or special homework/task log (refer to Daily Homework Log in the appendix, page 179). Have parents sign these agendas/logs on a nightly basis. The effective teacher checks for these signatures/initials to reinforce accountability. Think of the clout you have at a parent conference when discussing a student's lack of homework and responsibility with a parent who does not sign off on this log.

For the second time, use a class page on the Internet. List daily homework assignments as well as upcoming due dates for tests and projects. Remember the idea we mentioned earlier about using an incentive for reading this page? Choose a fun icon or catchy phrase that the student can share the following day either orally or written to receive extra credit or a bead/token.

As for the third opportunity to remind both parent/students of due dates or materials needed, refer to the cover letter of weekly/biweekly folders. Use bullets or bold words; keep reminders simple and spaced.

- *Acclamations.* When students are working very hard or performing well, they need to hear about their success. So do the parents. Everyone loves recognition especially when effort has been put into making the success happen. The effective teacher can easily drop a quick note into the weekly/biweekly folder; use a friendly premade form that requires a comment or two about Johnny's success. E-mails work well, too! Quantity doesn't matter here; it's quality in a few short words that we're after.
- *Written Correspondence.* All written communication should be professional and use a tone of encouragement—regardless of the content. Your intention is to relate not to overload your reader. The Edutainer understands that she is a motivator to both the student and parent. Respect and appreciation are front and center in all communication. Consider the following tips when using any written correspondence with your parents.
  ○ Keep writing simple and to the point. Bullets or columns make for good "quick reads."
  ○ Use factual language that is accurate and objective. Feelings are subjective. Avoid sarcasm and jokes that could easily be misunderstood. This is a professional, not a social, relationship.

- Tone should be professional yet easy to understand. Save your educational terminology for colleagues.
- Avoid all capital letters, as it expresses shouting, or difficult fonts, as they convey a "cutesy" manner. Colored text is touchy; remember red signals urgency or anger.
- Most important information should appear first or possibly in a subject line of a memo or e-mail.
- Always respond to or at least acknowledge a contact within twenty-four hours. Procrastination may only escalate a situation. Even if you don't have an immediate answer, acknowledge the request and inform the parent that you are looking into the solution.
- Be clear with any response or action that you want to follow the communication or that you, yourself, will be committing.
- Proofread and spell check. It is easy to use the wrong word or to misspell words. Trust and respect for your professionalism and leadership are quickly lost with these deadly blunders.
- Content that is confidential or controversial is better left to a meeting. Remember any information put into writing can show up on the front page of a newspaper or in legal documentation.

Documentation of Communication

One of the most tedious yet essential aspects of maintaining parent contact is keeping records of all written and oral communication. Seems easy enough to jot down who, when, and what was discussed. However, given that this interaction happens randomly throughout the teaching day, shreds of messages and important information become lost, or worse, the information never materializes. Enter the record keeping of an effective teacher.

We use a simple binder named "Parent Contact Log." This notebook is set up alphabetically including the name of every student that we teach. It is also a three-ring binder, so papers can easily be added or deleted as needed. Behind the student's name is a sheet of paper that includes important information received during a phone call (see Parent Contact Sheet in the appendix, pages 164–65). There is a place for the parent/guardian with whom

---

DID YOU KNOW . . . There were an estimated 210 billion e-mails sent per day in 2008.

we shared conversation, the date, important information discussed, and the outcome of the conversation.

E-mails, memos, and notes from home are also placed within this notebook. Messages left on voice mails can even be jotted down here. Just remember to complete the outcome or how you responded to this message. The papers are easily hole-punched and placed behind the corresponding student.

It's that easy—one place for all information for one student. Conference documentation, which we will refer to in the following pages of this chapter, is also placed here. How does this system have a no-fail guarantee? Never pick up the phone without it. And don't forget to include that surprise parent stopping at the door or a quick exchange that transpires in the hallway. Simply get into the routine of using the notebook.

Keeping/Sharing Grades
As we discussed with the concept of curriculum, the effective teacher must make choices for her students. The texts that are selected for a particular grade are only *tools* that the effective teacher uses. They are not in any form or fashion what determines the curriculum. The same thinking can be applied to grading. Everything a student is asked to do does not constitute a formal grade. The effective teacher understands the difference between introducing/practicing drills and actual performance assignments. The effective teacher would decide before any planning as to what she will consider in determining a student's grade.

- Daily grades—for example, class work and homework
- Quiz grades
- Test grades
- Projects

Moreover, the student and parent should be informed in advance as to how much each category weighs in the process of determining the course grade. This is to be shared in the open house meeting. Make sure to stress being proactive versus reactive. Don't encourage "Well, had we known" thinking during conference time. The Edutainer keeps her parents informed at all times during the school year.

Number grades are our choice of record keeping versus percentages. They are much easier to add and average. Parents understand a flat "80" versus a given percentage correct on an assignment and then trying to determine what percent this particular assignment weighs in on an entire grade of spelling or math.

Here are some strategies for simple grade keeping.

- Determine a set place and time of collecting assignments as discussed in our idea of establishing and reinforcing routines.
- Determine a proper heading, for example, name, student number, date, title of assignment, and page number.
- List each student alphabetically under every subject for which he will be receiving a grade.
- Student number is assigned to each student by alphabetical listing in the grade book. If Johnny is the fourth person in the order of the grade book, then he receives number four and will write this number under his name on all work. This system allows you to move methodically and quickly to determine what assignments are missing and how quickly scores can be entered into the grade book. Sort the papers in correct order before attempting to load each into the grade book, or add as a weekly job assigned to a student.
- When recording grades in a grade book, use pencil. Some teachers like the idea of color-coding, for example, red for tests, projects, or for late grades.
- When inputting grades into the computer from a grade book, use a highlighter to show grades that have been loaded versus the ones that still need to be put into the electronic grade book.
- Determine how often you will need to collect, grade, and record grades in the book. Will daily, weekly, or biweekly work best for you? Are you going to take ten or thirty grades per grading period? This will determine how frequently a student's work will be graded. Remember, not everything a student is asked to do will need a grade. Can the work be "checked" to simply see the assignment was practiced? Can the class use the assignment as a review? Does the work need to be evaluated item-by-item? You are the effective teacher; you decide. Keep in mind that assignments need to be meaningful, and students must be accountable for their responsibility that has been given.
- Determine a system that represents missing vs. absent papers. We like using an underscore in the box for missing or late work and a box for absent work. When the work is received or graded, you'll know how to determine a fair grade if points need to be deducted. This system also comes in handy when conferencing with parents. It is easy to see late grades when marked with an underscore, as it quickly draws attention to the times a student has been late with his responsibility.

- Determine how frequently grades/averages will be shared with both the student and parents. School systems typically use a quarter or semester time frame to send home formal report cards. An effective teacher issues "midway" reports that inform parents of their student's success about halfway through a grading period (see Quarterly Progress Report in the appendix, page 191).
- Grades and study habits as well as social skills can be addressed during this time. Again, don't wait for the final report to be sent home. Allow students the time and parents the knowledge to improve during the grading period. This form requires the parent signature and is returned. Be sure to file it in the "Parent Contact Log."
- The Edutainer chooses to incorporate extra effort in communicating both successful and less-than-satisfactory averages. Why? Students who are aware of their averages tend to be more productive in enhancing them, and parents want to know how their child is doing at all times throughout the year. If a child maintained a 78 average in a class, the effective teacher could pull this student aside and encourage him that with a bit more effort, he could possibly obtain an 80 or "B" average by mid-semester. However, if the student is unaware of his current average, little effort would be made to improve it. You're probably wondering exactly when you will have the time to do all this. And it is not that time consuming.
- If you are keeping up with your grading and inputting these grades in some type of electronic grade book, it only takes a few minutes one or two class times to pull individual students over to commend them for their excellent grades or privately encourage them to spend more time with homework or possibly studying for a test. The Edutainer is a partner in the education process, and this is a great way to lend a quick hand in sharing student's progress versus final destination.
- In the past, we often called this the "Leader of the Pack" announcements. With the students' permission, we would announce the highest current average in a given class. The students would often beg to hear the top three or, if uncomfortable about an average, would come up privately and ask to see his. Either way, encouragement or motivation can quickly be shared without waiting until the end of a grading period. Rewards were also shared during this time such as beads/bucks or candy to make it fun.
- Always have your grade book handy when meeting with a parent during a conference. Be organized, prepared, and professional. Most important, communicate.

Parent Conferences

Parent/teacher conferences are a wonderful opportunity for parents to see and hear information from you firsthand. Welcome this occasion and see it as an opportunity to "show them your stuff." You're the expert; let them experience that knowledge for themselves. During this face-to-face time, parents will be able to see how organized you are and how much thought you have put into your teaching. Their child is the beneficiary of all of your time and efforts.

We can share countless stories after parent conference days about parents who walk away "really understanding" how easy our classroom routines and expectations are. We have made huge headway when it comes to clarifying homework and class work expectations. So where is the disconnect? Life is hectic, families have more than one child, extracurricular activities keep even the most organized and functional families scrambling. Even with all of your organization and preparation in the beginning of the year, the light bulb waits to "come on" during a one-to-one meeting such as a parent-teacher conference.

So, get ready and look forward to what we refer to as some good ol' "station identification" time. Consider the following for setting up a successful parent/teacher conference (sample Conference Forms in the appendix, pages 192–98):

- Consider how you are going to have the parents sign up for the conference. Will you be assigning the time slot for that day or are parents given the opportunity to sign up for specified time slots? Give ample time for parents to schedule and rearrange their commitments to make themselves available.
- Determine how much time is needed for conferences. We suggest a fifteen- to twenty-minute time frame with five minutes in between each. This allows you to transition from one conference to the next and builds in extra time if needed.
- Have a backup plan for when parents are not able to attend on a specific day. Consider other days, times, and a strategy for when a parent needs to schedule a conference when it is not during a set conference day for all teachers.
- Determine how the room will be used. Arrange a table or cluster of desks at which you and the parents will be seated. Do not sit behind your teacher desk, as this creates a barrier. You want to present yourself as a team player, rather than "I am the teacher, and you are the student's parent." Everyone will be an equal party to the conference. Have a copy

of each text available, so that you can refer to it if needed. It gets confusing for parents to keep up with all of the materials that their child uses. Also determine where the next parent will sit while waiting if he or she arrives early or if the conference runs a bit late. Should the parent knock upon arrival? If so, post a sign. Consider having some work for the parents to browse such as class projects or other items to share.

- Have your record book, computer printouts of grades, and files organized in the order of conferences. Avoid embarrassing moments of not being able to locate a student's grade/work because it was placed out of order. Keep a copy of the conference schedule in front of you and a clock to keep you on time. Be ready to jot notes during the conference. Have Parent Contact Log handy.

- Plan a general but flexible outline of topics you would like to discuss during the conference.

- Consider sending parents a quick conference reminder and a few questions about some ideas they might like to discuss.

- Know whom you are meeting with—especially in divorced families. Don't assume names or roles.

- Greet the parents with a firm handshake, good eye contact, and an enthusiastic smile. Explain how you would like to structure the conference. Allow them to begin with any questions; for topics, refer to a preconference sheet the parent previously completed.

- Use the "sandwich" technique. Begin with positive comments; discuss areas that are of concern or need to be addressed; finish by saying something kind about the child's personal traits or abilities.

- Be specific in your observations and comments. Give the parents examples of what you are trying to explain. Have examples of the student's work to show strengths and weaknesses. This is really helpful when you're trying to convey a pattern that you've noticed in the student's assignments.

- Don't monopolize all the conversation. Allow the parents to share and ask questions. Ask for their opinions and observations. Stay focused and know you have a limited amount of time.

- Remember to incorporate the tools of good communication. Watch both verbal and nonverbal cues. Be positive and use active listening skills. Repeat what you have heard to be sure you understand what the parent is saying. For example, "I feel that you're saying . . ." Be cognizant of body language.

- Remember your counselor or other resource options in your school. Suggest the idea of referring them to this person(s) to further the investigation of helping their child.

- Offer suggestions or a course of action that would help the student to better his work habits and/or grades. Share tangible handouts that could help parents support their children at home. This is something that they can review later for themselves and/or with the student.
- Jot down notes—keep it brief; you can add details later; confirm the actions that you have agreed upon to help the student. Be clear both the parent and you understand the goal(s) moving forward if an action plan was made. Many teachers use a carbon paper that allows both the parent and teacher to have a brief document of the meeting.
- Review the main points; end the meeting on a positive note. Thank the parent for their time and support. Remind them that you are here if they need you.
- If you feel it might be helpful or even necessary, send the parents a brief e-mail summarizing the conference and thanking them for both their support and time. Express your enjoyment with meeting them personally and your anticipation of working together as a team in the future.

Portfolios

Another easy way to organize a student's work is by using a portfolio. This is simply a collection of student work completed throughout a given grading period or the entire year. It can contain both formal and informal assessments. The portfolio usually consists of writing samples, daily work in a variety of subjects, and tests. Both class and standardized testing can be filed here. It can be student and teacher selected work. Work can be returned to this folder just as easily as the weekly folder sent home.

From time to time, the student can be given the opportunity to select his best piece of work. Students usually have some type of reflective activity attached to this selection process that allows them the opportunity to explain "why" this piece of work is the best representation of his learning.

The portfolio is an easy way to share the students' progress over the year, too. Many teachers use portfolios as the basis for a class celebration. Here, parents are invited into the classroom with their children to share individual portfolios. Success is celebrated as a class but is also very individualized for the student with his parents (see Portfolio Suggestions in the appendix, page 199).

Communication is crucial at every level of the educational process. From the principal to the janitor, each individual who arrives at school every day is there to support the students' education. Student and parent communication are also vital components to any successful learning program. Students must feel a connection before they are able to process new information. Thus, effective communication affords students to make meaningful associations and to personalize information for authentic learning to take place. Furthermore, parents cannot support what they do not know.

Effective communication with parents allows them to feel connected and provides a chance to become involved and supportive in their child's education. The Edutainer enjoys the opportunity to help her students grow while learning and celebrating these milestones with her parents. Why, the entire cast both on and off stage celebrates a production well done!

SCENE 7

Edutainment

Education is not filling a bucket but lighting a fire.

—William B. Yeats

Have you have seen the show *Are You Smarter than a Fifth Grader?* It is designed for a contestant to answer questions that are derived from of a first-through fifth-grade curriculum. The object is to get to the million-dollar question, which is still only on a fifth-grade level. Well, as of this writing, there has been only one individual to actually answer the million-dollar question correctly, and she is the state school superintendent of Georgia. The interesting aspect is that there have been contestants on the show ranging from a nuclear engineer, professor, lawyer, astronaut, and everything in between. So, why didn't one of these individuals win the million dollars?

After all, they are successful in their chosen careers and yet still couldn't answer enough elementary level questions to win the game. Now, if you were a child watching the show, it might make you wonder exactly why you need to know the middle name of Richard Nixon? And as a teacher it does make you wonder if our current curriculum is actually relevant to the needs of students to function in our present-day culture or if it is just information that would help you on a quiz show. Should the goal of education be to simply inundate the students with information to memorize, or perhaps is it time to focus on application of information that will allow them to become productive citizens?

Our culture has changed so dramatically over the past few decades that the nature of the learning has changed as well. In the pre-Internet days, students relied on the teacher as their main source of information. The teacher had to "data dump" as much information as possible because students had limited access outside of the school setting. However, today students have unlimited access to information. But today in the information age, focus of education needs to be directed toward the application of knowledge.

This change is one reason that antiquated learning styles and teaching methods are often not successful in today's educational environment. Think of a strategy such as direct instruction, which is a highly scripted method of presenting information. This is "prepackaged" type of curriculum where everything is scripted out for the teachers and the student. This type of strategy is still widely used today. The problem that we see with this type of instruction is that it is a disservice to the students.

Yes, there are proponents and critics who argue about its effectiveness. But when you ask where in real life would this be replicated, well, it fails miserably. The reason some of these strategies work initially is that there is a focus given to a content area, such as reading. However, any strategy would show some improvement when emphasis is placed on the subject area. But do these strategies meet the demands of learning in today's culture?

The success of a strategy is measured by its ability to be valid, reliable, and sustainable. Many of these initiatives and strategies typically fall short in these areas, particularly their sustainability. The problem is that the "here today and gone tomorrow" mindset isn't effective for a changing culture. Another major flaw of many initiatives is that they don't ultimately place the responsibility of learning on the student.

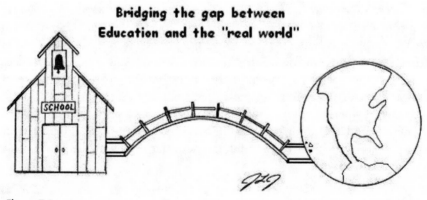

Figure 7.1.

Enter the Edutainment philosophy. If learning is deemed valuable and important to the student, then the educator doesn't need a scripted curriculum or a fad initiative that has students and the educator jumping through hoops. Edutainment is the philosophy through which we make the learning process relevant and applicable to the "real world" of the twenty-first century. Edutainment bridges the gap between traditional school and the real world. When this gap is bridged, students not only realize the relevance of education but will also take ownership of their learning.

Dolphins, Kids, and Other Mammals

Dolphins and Kids

Have you ever been to a dolphin show? You know, the one where the dolphin can jump twenty feet into the air and touch a ball with its nose, or find rings tossed thirty feet underwater with its eyes blindfolded? How did these dolphins get so smart? Does it mean the mammal has developed some higher-order reasoning skills to think through the process of finding the rings or even touching the ball in the air? Hardly, but it does mean it was conditioned to do the activity.

The reinforcement for the dolphins is typically a bucket of raw fish. The dolphins are trained to jump through hoops just as students are trained to jump through hoops. The hoops students have to jump through are exams, quizzes, and standardized tests, all in the hopes of passing each class and eventually graduating from school. And remember the direct instruction? That is where the teacher reads from a script, and then activates a stimulus to which the students respond. The only thing missing is a fish for the students when they respond correctly.

Conditioning in and of itself is not necessarily a bad thing. There are many factors both intrinsically and extrinsically that motivate. Conditioning can also include rewards or punishment, as both shape students' behavior. That is why it is important to have clearly defined consequences for your rules and why expectations are important to defining student behavior as well. Rewards such as the beads or class bucks do have a place in the learning environment although these should not be the foundational motivations of the learning environment. Yes, everyone enjoys being rewarded occasionally; even adults seek extrinsic rewards. However, the ultimate goal of the Edutainer is for the student to be intrinsically motivated.

Other Mammals

It is not just student learning that is conditioned. Do you realize that most of our daily routine is a result of habit or conditioning? Remember Pavlov's dogs? They were conditioned to respond to a stimulus. While we like to think as humans we are above this type of conditioning, we really aren't. Take the golden arches for instance, which is one of the most recognized symbols in the world. Yet McDonald's still spends millions of dollars each year on advertising. Why, you may ask? Because they know if you see enough commercials, you will be conditioned to stop by because you "deserve a break today."

Why is it important to understand that many of our behaviors are habits formed through conditioning?

You probably have a teaching routine that you do without even realizing it. It might not be the most effective way to reach your students, but you have been conditioned over time and do it without even thinking. This reinforces our belief that when someone claims "I have twenty years of experience," it really means that they have had twenty years of the same experience. For example, a teacher may say "I have twenty years of experience in teaching math," when in reality they have taught math using the same methods for twenty years. This means there has been limited adaptation or growth.

So, one important skill utilized by the Edutainer is to adapt to the current needs of the students. It is all too simple to fall into a routine because it is comfortable and established. However, another word for this type of delivery is *stale*. An entertainer is not effective if she is using the exact same routine or act that she used two or three years ago. An entertainer is constantly updating material and delivery for maximum results.

In most instances the method of delivery is by lecture. As you learned in the communication chapter, only 7 percent of words are remembered, so the most used method of delivery is actually the least effective. Even when visual aids are included, the focus is mainly on the lecture itself. This is because it is comfortable or a routine for most teachers to use this method of delivery for information. So what changes need to be made for teaching and learning to be most effective in the twenty-first century?

Performing in the Twenty-First Century

The education a child receives needs to be applicable to the world beyond the school building. This task would include graduating students who are able to function in society, not just recite poetry or name the capitals of the fifty states. Gone are the days where the "A" students were the ones who could memorize the most information; here and now are the days that require mastery of higher-order thinking skills such as evaluation and application.

In this changing culture there appears to be easy access to information, but a lack of ability to retain the information long-term, or the ability to use the information in a practical manner. How many students can balance a checkbook, or understand how to purchase something as practical as a car? To help maximize learning in the twenty-first century here are a few important components to consider.

Relevance

It is human nature to take an interest in things that are relevant to our own lives. Since practically every aspect of education is in some way relevant to students' lives, it is important for the teacher to make the connection because you can't assume that the students will make the connection of the relevance by themselves. Lily Eskelsen (vice president of the NEA) explains, "You have to have a mastery of what you're teaching, and you have to present it in a way that captures the attention of kids who don't necessarily appreciate the relevance of the subject in their immediate lives.

"Your presentation skills are what make you a teacher and not just a researcher, writer, or a pontificator of facts and opinions. You are a performer and the best performers ENGAGE their audience—they have a sense of whether or not the audience is 'with them' or, if they've lost them, they know how to 'focus them and lead them.'"

Do you remember when you were in school and some students in algebra class complained, "When will we ever use this information?" Well, some students still ask the relevance of the information they are learning today. In reality, algebra is used in everyday life. The key is to connect the math curriculum with real life application so the students can see the similarities. First, remember that algebra is about variables, and life is all about variables as well.

Real-life variables involve:

- Choosing what kind of car I need to buy
- Analyzing and forecasting profit of a business
- Determining how many bags of hotdog buns are needed for a party in relation to the number of hotdogs purchased
- Budgeting for a trip: gas prices vs. mileage, hotel costs vs. number of nights, etc.

Motivation

Students are exposed to more information by the age of five than their grandparents were exposed to by the age of twenty. So the issue is not a lack of information but rather a lack of motivation. Through the Internet, iPods, cell phones, and other technology, students have continual access to information. Because of this access, many students aren't motivated much beyond simply finding information.

As several of our interviews revealed, students today aren't very motivated to work hard. There is a sense of entitlement, where students think simply by showing up or turning in "any" work should be acceptable. This is where your high expectations will help them understand that turning in "anything" is not acceptable. The Edutainer sets a high standard for what is acceptable and what is not. Consider these strategies for motivating the students as you start the school year.

- Use tools in technology that the students know how to use. It will build self-esteem and motivate them as well since it is a familiar format of information. If teachers don't use technology because they are not proficient in it, allow the students be the experts.
- Reinforce hard work with public praise and occasionally a reward or privilege.
- Provide opportunities for a variety of experiences, like field trips.
- Make lessons as applicable to the real world as possible, such as using grocery shopping for math content.
- Make students active participants in learning, such as making videos or teaching class themselves.
- Treat students with respect.
- Inspire students to do their best. Students really do want to succeed.

Stage Presentation
One aspect of learning that is essential to the Edutainer is in presentation of the material. Two different teachers can give the same information, but if one teacher presents the information in an enthusiastic or dynamic manner, the information will be more relatable.

If culture plays as large a role as research suggests in learning, then why is the classroom the only place where students are so confined and restricted in their methods of learning. Has anyone thought that this may be why students are often disconnected in the classroom?

Do you make them sit at a desk at home to learn a new song? And in what business profession would you find workers sitting in rows? We are not suggesting that there shouldn't be order in the classroom, but maybe the learning environment needs to be more suited to real life.

A perfect example of this concept is a study that was done with children and food. Children were given food such as carrots in a plain wrapper and then they were given carrots wrapped in a McDonald's wrapper. Guess which carrots the children thought tasted better? You guessed it, the ones in the McDonald's wrapper. It was all in the presentation. Food in a McDonald's wrapper had to taste better, because after all, it is McDonald's!

So, create an environment where students can move, be creative, and actually enjoy learning.

- Place beanbags or chairs in the room where students can read. This gives them opportunity to get out from behind desk during the day.
- Play classical music when students are working independently or writing activities.
- Build a stage for presentations. Examples in classrooms we have seen or used include tree houses and even an actual castle complete with a tower where students would present book talks.
- Interchange activities that allow for movement around the classroom (see intermission 2).
- Make the learning environment more inviting. Incorporate technology, put up colorful posters, use different lighting or sound in a performance. It's all in the presentation.

Thinking Globally
The Edutainer understands the necessity of global education. As other countries enter the global economy, students have to be prepared for working in a diverse culture. However, cultural diversity isn't just necessary for interacting with other countries. The United States has by far the highest immigration rate in the world. Since our own society is rich in diversity, there are challenges as well as opportunities that are associated with being the most culturally diverse educational system in the world.

As an effective educator, embrace the cultural diversity of your classroom. Remember, regardless of their background, students desire and deserve to learn in an effective learning environment. Therefore, develop a sense of understanding and value for all students in the classroom. Each student brings a uniqueness and personality to the class community. Embracing cultural diversity can even include partnering with a school in a different country, so you can understand and appreciate their culture.

Remember to focus on the three Rs, since they are integral to twenty-first-century education. These are important for creating a safe, respectful, and productive working environment for all students.

- *Relevance*. Students find the information applicable to their own lives.
- *Relationship*. Students feel a sense of community or belonging. Individuals who feel connected to the classroom will perform at a higher level.
- *Responsibility*. Students have a responsibility to be respectful and helpful to everyone in the classroom. You, as the Edutainer, model the expected student behavior.

Finally, there are certain needs that all people, regardless of ethnicity or culture have in common. These three needs can actually be summed up in the three Rs that are the foundational underpinning to the edutainment philosophy. It is in these areas of commonality that create a safe and engaging environment for all students.

- Utilize as many learning styles as you can to meet the students' needs.
- Use a variety of teacher- and student-centered activities.
- Incorporate information from other cultures, for example, by communicating with schools in another country.
- Always be consistent with expectations, consequences, and even rewards.

The Joy of Learning

We spend the first twelve months of our children's lives teaching them to walk and talk and the next twelve telling them to sit down and shut up.

—Phyllis Diller

Learning is an important characteristic of human behavior. Think of how babies crawl on the floor looking for objects, which then go directly into their mouths. At first glance you would think the baby is hungry, or, as Freud thought, there is an oral fixation. In reality, the baby is simply exploring and learning. Adults often hamper the inquisitive nature of children as well. What is the first thing a young couple does when having a baby? They "baby proof" their homes. Basically, they want the child to sit still in one place all day so he doesn't harm himself.

Isn't that what we have done in schools as well? "Child proofed" the schools? We want students to sit still in one place all day, so they don't harm themselves or others. And then we wonder why they don't enjoy learning.

Children learn through many media, which can actually involve playing and having fun at times. Even brain-based research suggests that learning is enhanced when children are moving and active. This is a far cry from most classrooms, where students must sit still, which is in contradiction to their inquisitive and exploring nature.

That's why children start school with "wide-eyed wonder," excitement, and a desire for new experiences, but typically by fourth grade, school has become a boring routine.

So, make learning engaging and, yes, even fun. Learning can be enjoyable and satisfying even when it requires much work. Much like your job, learning is hard work, but at the end of the day the work produces a sense of satisfaction. When we taught life science, we didn't like to be confined to the classroom. Science should be experienced, not just taught. So, the students would go outdoors for class. These nature tours brought science and students together in a way that couldn't be achieved in the classroom.

For instance, when the students were learning about plants, they would learn how to identify trees by their leaves, bark, or the fruit/nut that they produced rather than simply relying on texts or paper materials limited to the classroom. The students would be so excited that they would tell the other classes about it during lunch or break. The daily lesson became exciting and memorable.

As you can see, teaching and learning in the twenty-first century is very different from even twenty years ago. The information age, globalization, and culture in general have created a gap between the real world and antiquated education. The effective educator understands the importance of providing relevant and practical teaching today. She also understands that the foundation for success is the relationships built by and with the students. Before we leave this section, here are some tips for surviving in the twenty-first century culture.

Tiers of Instruction

A good teacher is a master of simplification and an enemy of simplism.

—Louis Berman

Much focus has been on the Edutainer, and with good reason—she is the most important influence on student learning. However, the success of the student in the real world ultimately rest on his own shoulders. It is the student, after all, who has to learn how to use the information he has learned and make it applicable to future learning and life in general. Therefore, we have developed the "tiers of instruction," which are the foundational principles of the

Tips for performing in a twenty-first century culture:

- *Adaptability.* Times change, and learning should be fluid to adjust to changing culture. Be flexible and adjust the presentation of information to maximize learning.
- *Relationships.* Develop and nurture authentic relationships. When there is a real sense of community everyone is working toward common goals rather than disconnected individual pursuits.
- *Relevance.* Connect with the students and connect the content with their lives. Relevant teaching is effective teaching.
- *Responsibility.* Create an environment of personal responsibility, classroom (group) responsibility, and social responsibility (acting responsibly with the interests of the larger community in mind).
- *Communication.* Understanding, managing, and creating effective oral, written, and multimedia communication.
- *Core skills.* Effectively plan, organize, and manage your stage, performance, and cast. This requires an educator that has self-confidence and feels empowered.
- *Reflection.* Like a performer, an Edutainer reflects upon her performance to focus on areas of success and improvement. Remember, awareness of self and your habits are important to effective change.

Edutainment philosophy. The tiers of instruction allow the responsibility of learning to transition from the effective educator to the student.

Many learning and instructional theories contain numerous principles and levels of learning. Maybe that's why we refer to them as the "tears of instruction." This is not to disregard theories such as Bloom's taxonomy or Merrill's principles of instruction design, but these often appear most effective in theory, and the sheer volume of them can make them impractical. Practicality is the key, since we are, after all, dealing with real students in the real world.

These theories seem especially burdensome when you have to consider them on top of the curriculum, differentiated learning, multiple intelligences, and other aspects of learning. In fact, by the time you consider all of the known theories and principles of learning that might go into a lesson, you would probably prefer to participate in the "running of the bulls" in Pamplona.

However, if brevity is indeed the soul of wit, then it is our contention that "simplicity is the soul of genius." The Edutainer utilizes only three tiers of instruction to move learning from a teacher-centered approach to a student-centered approach where the student owns his learning. The tiers of instruction are fluid, individualized, and take into account the relevance of a changing culture. Each stage represents an integral part of the learning process and ultimately transitions the responsibility of learning from the educator to the student, as the student takes ownership of his learning. The tiers of instruction include the following three stages:

- *Foundation.* Presenting new material to students in such a manner that material can be recalled.
- *Personalization.* Personalizing the information, so that it can be absorbed, retained, and utilized.
- *Transformation.* Responsibility of internalizing and integrating information is transferred from Edutainer to the student.

The following chart explains the three tiers as well as the role of the Edutainer and student in each stage. The responsibility of learning is transitioned from the effective educator to the student as the stages progress. The tiers of instruction chart offers the goals of each stage and objectives for the student. (See figure 7.2.) This chart serves as a handy reference for novice teachers in introducing and building on a lesson.

Applying the Tiers of Instruction

Applying the tiers of instruction to a lesson requires planning. However, once this approach is used, the effective teacher can create a more relevant curriculum. Through this planning, students will become more engaged and eventually take ownership of their learning as the stages progress. We will now examine the stages and provide strategies for maximizing each level for optimal student success.

Foundation

The foundation stage is the first stage of instruction. Simply put, this is where the Edutainer introduces new material and builds a foundation for personalized learning. Unfortunately, this tier utilizes most of the instructional time in the average classroom. Many teachers simply begin with the curriculum they have been given and hope to finish it by the end of the year. When faced with so much content to cover, it is understandable why teachers simply present information and then move on to the next topic.

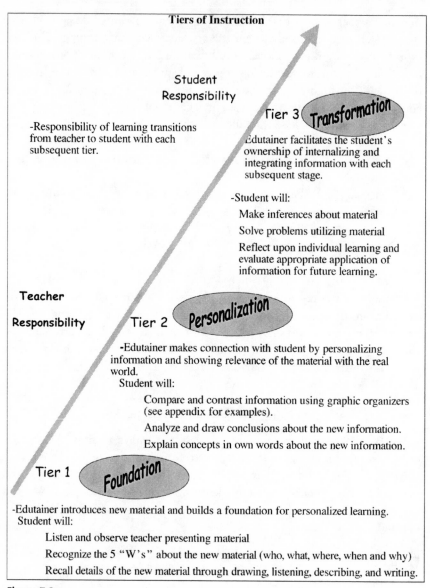

Figure 7.2.

Unfortunately, this type of instruction does not lend itself to any depth of knowledge where the students can personally absorb the information and make it relevant to future learning. As we discussed in the planning chapter, curriculum must be mapped and prioritized with state and national standards to eliminate holes and avoid "data dumping" for the sake of simply covering content.

If the next level is not achieved, then the information presented in this stage will at best be memorized short-term and then quickly forgotten. Again, the Edutainer understands the responsibility of relevant learning lies upon her. If the student doesn't see relevance or connection, then the opportunity to learn will be missed. Here are sample questions you can ask for formal or informal feedback. The foundation stage mainly emphasizes the five Ws of the information (who, what, where, when, and why).

- Who is the main character?
- Can you recall . . . ?
- Can you define or describe . . . ?
- What happened first? (Create a timeline.)
- List some of the important happenings . . . map ideas.
- Make lists of details using a chart.

Personalization

The second tier requires more active learning on the part of the student beyond simply listening while the Edutainer disperses information. For information to be absorbed, it has to possess worth and relevance to the students. When information is presented in a relevant and applicable manner, it allows the students to absorb the information more effectively. Therefore, this stage requires personalization of the information. The effective educator must make the material relatable to the students so they retain the information as important and useful. In this stage the Edutainer uses humor, shares stories, or utilizes activities that the students will find interesting.

The following are strategies you may want to consider when students are providing feedback on new material. Keep in mind that you want to connect the material to the real world, so feedback should reflect it as well.

Students will:

- Make comparisons and contrasts of information using a Venn diagram.
- Make predictions of outcomes while reading a novel or before completing a science lab.
- Relate material with own experiences. Write and share personal connections with lesson theme.
- Apply learning to cultural issues. Create a commercial or product related to the lesson.

Transformation

The final tier transitions the ownership of learning from the Edutainer to the students. When students are able to take ownership of learning, they become good decision makers. In this stage, students begin to understand the relevance of learning or "why" they must learn something. The goal of the *transformation stage* is to help students utilize their knowledge through reflective thinking. With such a focus on standardized testing and covering content, we are currently teaching our students that information alone is important, when in reality the student needs to reflect upon what he knows and what he needs to do with it.

Learning in isolation or without connection to the student is learning that is not utilized long-term; it becomes dead. Zach Young (head of Wesleyan School), when asked about the weakness of education in today's culture, replied, " Students today have access to more information, but they still lack discernment . . . many lack the ability to make wise decisions."

This stage focuses upon advanced thinking skills, which are important for those who will enter the twenty-first-century workforce. This workforce will require individuals who are flexible, dynamic, and resilient. The effective teacher employs a great deal of inventiveness and "connectedness" in designing lessons that meet the dual challenge of providing the basics and developing the ability to reason. Consider these strategies that support the transition from teacher-centered to student-centered learning.

Students will:

- Make judgments about new information by evaluating the pros and cons of an issue.
- Reflect upon personal understanding of material. Reorganize main concepts through graphic organizers, writing composition, or developing flow chart.
- Debate the relevance or validity of material by preparing a list of criteria or conduct a debate about an issue from the lesson.
- Create a presentation or product to show how the lesson applies to another situation.

One activity that we had students do in a health/fitness class was to create a family health tree. This is similar to a family tree but instead of just listing relatives they included any diseases/illnesses that existed within their family. For instance, if a student's grandmother had cancer, the student would place her in the appropriate spot and list cancer as a disease. If she had other diseases, then those would be added as well. After the student constructed the tree, he would examine it to determine the most common illnesses. As an opportunity to reflect upon the activity, students would write a report discussing the top two or three diseases and ways to prevent those diseases in their own lives.

This activity was relevant and transformational because the students realized that the decisions they made affected their health based upon family history. An interesting bonus to this activity was the parent involvement. Regardless of whether it was a middle school student or a college student, the parents were just as interested as the students.

Characteristics of Transformational Learning

The characteristics of transformational learning are hinged upon relating education to the real world of the students. It is the bridging of this gap that makes learning applicable and desirable to the student. When students value and take ownership of their learning, then this gap has been bridged. Here are some of the characteristics of transformational learning:

- Learning is real-world oriented and has value beyond the school setting.
- Instruction uses hand-on approaches and is accessible for all learners.
- Allows students to collaborate on work.
- Produces a product that is directed toward a real audience.
- Gives opportunities for students to reflect upon their learning.

Since the focus of transformation learning is to place the responsibility of learning on the students, it is important to include the students in the learning process. Focus upon what will motivate them to take ownership of the educational process. Consider these tips for including students in the transformational learning process:

- *Let kids make decisions.* Kids today have more freedom and input into their own lives, unlike earlier generations. Children are consumers who make decisions about purchasing clothes, cell phones, video games, music, and much more. The Edutainer understands this shift of choice and tries to use it in the classroom whenever possible. For example, she would allow students choice of projects and opportunities to demonstrate their knowledge rather than the teacher deciding every detail within given parameters. Learning doesn't have to be robotic.
- *Invite students to publish for a broader audience.* For example, YouTube.
- *Incorporate a global audience.* Initiate a project with a peer classroom in a foreign country.

- *Focus on creation rather than consumption.* Take advantage of students hunger to create and innovate by allowing them to collaborate or develop their own materials, for example, PowerPoint, video clips, or even websites using educational templates.
- *Let them teach you about their world.* Allow your students to share technological tools that are part of their everyday life.
- *Scaffolding.* Allow students that are more proficient in a given content area to help other students who struggle.
- *Service projects/other-centered.* Find a charity or some other community organization and create a project for a class to do over the course of a month or even a semester (see intermission 1 for ideas).

Technology

Everything in our culture revolves around technology. We are obsessed with the "biggest and best" mentality whether it be a 102" widescreen, high-definition, plasma television or a super-deluxe microwave that can cook a whole cow in thirty seconds. This obsession with technology may be based upon the perception that the more technology you have, the better off you are. Even within education, there are individuals who think that technology in and of itself is the cornerstone of the learning process.

As we have illustrated throughout the chapters, technology and the "information age" have greatly influenced our culture. Whether it is the surround sound in a movie theater, the spectacular lighting of a concert, or the ability to surf the Internet from a cell phone, technology has changed how we obtain and utilize information.

Proper Perspective

While technology is important in today's culture, the Edutainer understands the role of technology as a *communication tool*. Technology conveys information, ideas, and concepts in an efficient manner. Much like an entertainer, who uses extravagant lighting, video, or sound, he understands it is only a small piece of the show and not the foundation of the performance. Therefore, when too much importance is placed on the "bells and whistles" of technology rather than sound methods of learning, it can actually be counterproductive to the educational environment. Ultimately, the Edutainer incorporates technology into her presentations, but she doesn't rely on it to be the core of her performance.

On the other extreme there are educators who resist using technology in the classroom. These individuals equate technology with playtime and

Figure 7.3.

leisure rather than learning. When they think of technology, it conjures up thoughts of loud music, video games, or even iPods permanently attached to a student's body. The problem with ignoring technology is that you limit yourself with tools for delivering information in a present-day style. As an Edutainer, you are aware that technology can greatly increase creativity and the relevance of a lesson.

If technology can be somewhat intimidating, here are a few tips to help you get started.

- Check with your school or school system to find out what courses are offered in technology. You can kill two birds with one stone. You can earn certification credit while you become comfortable with technology in a nonthreatening environment.
- Begin with simpler programs, such as PowerPoint to present a lesson.
- Allow students to teach the class about technologies they know well.
- Take a class on a new software program such as Dyknow.
- Spend time with technology. For instance, search the Internet for resources that can enhance the delivery of materials.

Not a Crutch

As wonderful as technology can be, there is also the potential for misuse. For example, one problem with technology is when it is used in place of sound teaching methodologies. As Chip Saltman (vice president of Cap Gemini) said, "In some instances technology is used as a crutch by teachers to take up time when they could be teaching a lesson." How many times have you heard of teachers letting students play on the computers rather than planning a productive lesson for the class? These teachers assume that any use of technology is validated, when in reality it may serve as a babysitter instead of a communication tool.

As a tool, technology does provide access to an abundance of knowledge. This leads to another problem with technology, where students assume any information is legitimate and credible. As Dr. Gary Preston explained, "Students today will access information on a Google search and will use it in their research papers even if it's not from a credible source . . . they aren't willing to take the time to seek out legitimate sources." This, however, may be a symptom of our culture beyond the school setting.

One poignant example is the sociology student who made national headlines. He wrote a fake quote and then attributed it to a French composer at the time of his death. A multitude of media outlets (television, newspapers, and magazines) attributed the quote to the French composer. No one took the time to check and see if the quote was legitimate. Only a couple of the news organizations researched and found the error, but many of them never admitted to the error.

Imagine, news organizations printing something as a fact without any foundation. Unfortunately, the Internet is often seen as indisputable—if it appears on the Internet, well, then it must be true. Therefore, it is our responsibility as educators to reinforce the importance of finding credible sources and information on the Internet. Students must be taught to verify that the information is indeed valid.

Maximizing Technology Tools

As we have expressed, communication technology is simply a tool for sharing information. However, it can be an efficient, powerful, and creative tool. Technology can be used in multiple methods, such as presenting basic information in a PowerPoint presentation or making a video with the class that relates a topic to the real world. As Kathy Cox indicated, "There isn't enough creativity in technology use . . . we are bound by software and other people's technology." As an Edutainer you want to maximize the opportunities that would allow for creative plans with technology.

Therefore, we offer these strategies and ideas to maximize your resourcefulness and creativity as you deliver a stellar performance.

- Utilize current online resources. United Streaming, for example, is a great resource for videos on any subject. These include videos by the history, health, and science channel. These clips can be as short as a few minutes or as lengthy as an hour. Use these to enhance your presentation; don't let it *be* the presentation.

- Incorporate music into the school day. Music is often a fundamental part of our lives, yet it is so often neglected in the typical classroom.
- Find quality reference or resource sites for yourself and students. For example, Questia is an excellent resource for books, professional journals, and magazines.
- Use concept-mapping software. Students can use them to create story maps, cause-and-effect diagrams, and flow charts. These are premade templates that are very user friendly.
- Utilize interactive technology tools such as Smart or active boards and Dyknow.

Education must make a connection to the real world to be relevant and applicable in the twenty-first century. It is no longer adequate to simply provide information to the students and expect them to make the connections in order to be successful. The Edutainment philosophy is fundamental to the educational process when it comes to personalizing and teaching relevant learning. This philosophy is the bridge that connects education to the twenty-first century.

Finale

Mary Dimino

If I could sum up all I've ever felt about teachers, it would be with this quote by Henry Brooks Adams: "A teacher affects eternity; he can never tell where his influence stops."

At first glance, one may not realize how much the educator and the entertainer are alike. But as a comedian, actress, and someone who has been greatly inspired by a few fantastic teachers in my life, I know all too well the similarities. I know that the core skills of being an effective performer are also the same core skills for being an effective teacher. When fellow comedians and thespians hit the stage, we use our skills, skills that were honed from years of learning our craft. We know that first and foremost, we need to come from a place of truth, a place of authenticity to the given circumstances and to ourselves. The good performer shows vulnerability, excitement, confidence, wit, and likability. The good performance is one in which a connection has been made and felt by the audience.

The good teacher, too, shows vulnerability, excitement, confidence, wit, and likability. The good lesson is one in which a connection has been made and felt by the students. These are the indistinguishable and most wonderful elements that motivate people to higher places. Connection is key. Performing five nights a week in the clubs of New York City, I know that keeping an audience's attention (especially an audience that has met or exceeded a two-drink minimum) is all about connection. It can be only too easy to lose an audience if they don't feel a sense of involvement or bond with you. This connection is exciting, even quite palpable.

Why do you think not many people volunteer to sit in the front row of a comedy club? They'll say they don't want to get "picked on." That is because there is no fourth wall in comedy. This isn't quite theater, in which the audience is a voyeur. No, in fact, it is exactly here where it is about connection, about the moment, about what is relevant in the room right here right, right now. You sneeze; the comic can say, "Bless you." You, in many ways, are a part of the show. Similarly, with teaching it is so important to include the students in the learning process, to focus upon what will motivate them to take ownership of their educational process.

Connection comes with eye contact, honesty, relatability, and a true sense of fun. The audience senses when the performer is not having fun or when the comic is just phoning it in that night. Making a connection, and the likability that comes with it, is what makes an audience interested in listening to what you have to say. Once you have 'em, you hit home your punch lines. In like manner, once a teacher has grasped a hold on a student's mind, inspiration occurs and miracles are made.

I personally love it when people approach me after a show and talk as if they've known me for years. It is such a pleasure to know that they feel so comfortable with me. They confide well-kept secrets, buy me drinks after the show, and even invite me to their home for Christmas dinner. It is truly amazing how you can touch someone's heart just by being real. This sense of approachability too, can be felt by the students and can make a difference in their lives. The teacher that exudes approachability is so very special, and so very needed.

The classroom of the twenty-first century is a unique place. Things are changing so fast around us, why shouldn't the classroom change, too? That is why I love the Edutainers; like entertainers, they too are continually seeking relevance. Entertainment, technology, and new media have come so far in the last twenty years, why shouldn't education? We would be amiss not to change with our times. Not changing can only lead to a lack of inspiration. And inspiration is what students need to be involved. By embracing advances in both technology and pop culture, teachers, like the comedians, can connect their messages with the real world. This is what makes education applicable to the lives of students. And this is what makes for fantastic teachers.

I still remember my teachers. I especially remember my Edutainers. Dear Mr. Sidlinger, teacher of seventh-grade English. His enthusiasm was contagious, sending ripples of influence through his students' lives. I'd be carried away with inquisitiveness for whatever he was talking about that day. He'd connect his lessons with stuff going on in his life, our lives, and the world. It intrigued me to see how subjects like English could be so relevant to everyday life.

What stood out most about Mr. Sidlinger was his vulnerability; always joking, never taking himself, or us for that matter, too seriously. He was the first teacher that made me realize that this whole "learning" thing can be pretty darn cool. His passion for connecting with his class sparked something in me. I have it to this day. Thank you, Mr. Sidlinger.

You, dear reader, are a person who will be remembered throughout your students' lives. Long after they marry, have kids, move away—you, your name, your face, your voice, your words will stay with them forever. Such influence, such power, such a beautiful ability to shape lives!

When my home club, Stand-Up New York, asked me to teach a comedy class, at first I declined. "Why in the world would I want to do that?" I asked myself. After much prodding by Carey Hoffman, the club owner, I reluctantly agreed. "It's only temporary, now," I'd say. Well, seven years later, I can't begin to express how blessed I feel every time a new class enrolls.

Months, even years after someone has studied with me, I'd get letters, e-mails, phone calls, visits of thanks. Gratitude that comes from such a deep, sincere place it nearly takes my breath away each time. They'd thank me for giving them confidence, for manifesting a desire they've held secretly inside their hearts for years, for getting them on stage and helping them write an act, for bringing the joy back to their lives, for making a dream come true. To think I was able to do that!

Wow, to inspire someone, not just entertain, but inspire also. That is why I teach. I've discovered that not only is teaching like performing, in some ways, it is better. It goes deeper. It is a privilege to hold such a special place in a person's heart and mind. If I can feel this way teaching a comedy workshop, I can only imagine how a true educator may feel. What fulfillment, what delight there is in connection!

In the end, the Edutainer doesn't need to be concerned so much that the student was entertained, but that a connection was made; a spark was lit. A gap was bridged between traditional learning and the realities of the world. It is here that the student will realize the relevance of education and will take ownership of their learning. Teaching means leaving a piece of yourself in the development of another. And the student is where we "deposit our most precious treasures."

I am both lucky and honored to know the authors of this book, Brad and Tammy, both professionally and as friends. They are true Edutainers. They have put every word of this book into practice. They, like you, are the hard-working, exquisite teachers of our time.

> Education is no longer an isolated profession. It needs to grow, like everything around it. Let it start with you.
>
> —Mary Dimino (comedian, actress, 2008 Gracie Allen Award Winner)

(Mary is a winner of the 2008 Gracie Allen Award presented by American Women in Radio and Television. The Gracie honors exemplary contributions of individuals who have encouraged the realistic and faceted portrayal of women in entertainment, commercials, and featured programming. Mary has appeared on *Comedy Central*, *David Letterman*, and *Conan O'Brien*, as well as in several commercial and television roles. She is currently on comedy tour with "The Italian Chicks" while also performing her own off-Broadway production *Scared Skinny*. She teaches classes for aspiring comedians at Stand-Up New York Comedy Club. Mary also serves on the advisory board of her alma mater, Hofstra University.)

Encore (Appendix)

Parent Contact Sheet

Student_____ Homeroom_____

Parents' names:

Mom_____ Dad_____

Address_____

_____

Student lives with _____

Home phone_____

Alternate numbers:

Mom's cell _____ Work_____

Dad's cell _____ Work _____

Email addresses:

Mom_____

Dad_____

Date	Student Behavior	Parent contacted	Comments	Outcome

Parent Contact Sheet

Student:_____ Grade_____

Homeroom:_____ Home telephone_____

Teacher:_____ Subject/period_____

Date	How Contacted	Reason for contact	Outcome

Student Survey Form

1. What are your child's major interests?

2. Describe your child's strengths. (Include academic, physical, and social strengths.)

3. What are your child's strongest academic subjects?

4. What are your child's weakest academic subjects?

5. Which academic areas would you like to see strengthened?

6. What should be your child's main academic goals for the first two weeks?

Name_____   Date_____

____ Grade
Missed You
A Bunch!

Science

Social Studies

English

Geography

Math

Spelling

Reading

Vocabulary

Writing

We're "Grapeful" For All of Your Hard Work...

Study Skills

Teacher:

_____

Substitute Teacher Folder Checklist

Please include the following in your substitute teacher folder:

- ❑ Emergency Notebook (includes class rolls, evacuation, fire, and tornado drills).

- ❑ Seating Charts with essential student information included.

- ❑ Copy of current lesson plans and suggested activities to reinforce concepts.

- ❑ Name of teacher as contact person for any questions.

- ❑ Your *daily procedures* (arrival, dismissal, lunch count, attendance, class routine and rules, etc.). Don't forget to include recess and playground procedures, hallway and bathroom rules, and computer rules, if they apply.

- ❑ Discipline Forms (referral forms).

- ❑ Classroom management plan and school discipline policies.

- ❑ A weekly schedule of daily specials and activities (encore classes, recess, etc.).

- ❑ If you team-teach or switch classes with another staff member, be sure to include that schedule as well. If you are going someplace special or have a special speaker coming, it should be noted in your lesson plans.

- ❑ Schedule and names of student who leave for — or —.

- ❑ Teaching Assistants and Special Education Staff—You also need to have a schedule listing who you work with, times you have specific students, and your plans for each area or student.

- ❑ Health concerns for your students.

- ❑ Access codes for you phone. (Be sure to leave instructions on how to get the messages off of your phone. Also include a number for the office.)

- ❑ Note whether or not you want the sub to correct papers that have been done in your class. Let them know how you want this handled. (They are told in the substitute orientation session that they are to correct papers unless they are told otherwise.)

- ❑ Leave the sub bottled water if you have a small fridge, or healthy snack.

KWLH Chart

What I Know	What I Want to Know	What I Learned	How I can Learn More

Name_____   Date_____

Name_____   Cluster Maps   Date_____

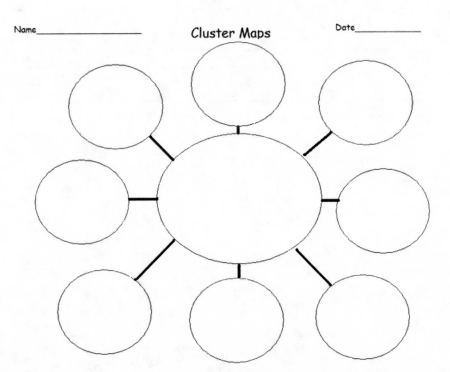

Name_____   **Sequencing Chart**   Date_____

First_____
_____
_____
_____
_____

Next _____
_____
_____
_____
_____

Then _____
_____
_____
_____
_____

Name_____   Date_____

Venn Diagram

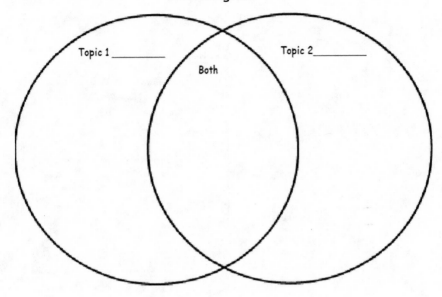

Name _____

Date_____

Cause and Effect Chart

Cause		Effect
		Effect
		Effect

Cause		Effect
		Effect
		Effect

- Identify an event or issue. Find the cause or causes by asking, why did this happen? Discover the effect or effects by asking, what happened as a result?

Name_____   Date_____

Reading Record

Title	Author	Genre	Number of pages.	Key idea or concept from the book

Word Study Boxes

Definition	Sentence
Word	
Synonym	Picture
Antonym	

Definition	Sentence
Word	
Synonym	Picture
Antonym	

Definition	Sentence
Word	
Synonym	Picture
Antonym	

Definition	Sentence
Word	
Synonym	Picture
Antonym	

Name_____   Date_____

5"W's"

Who is story about?

What happened in story?

Story or topic

Where did story take place?

When did story happen?

Why is story important?

How did events happen?

Student Supply List

- ❑ Two packs of #2 pencils
- ❑ Two packs of lined paper (wide ruled)
- ❑ Two highlighters (preferably yellow)
- ❑ Two red pens
- ❑ One pack of ink pens (blue and black)
- ❑ One pack of pencil top erasers
- ❑ One pack of Expo markers (basic colors)
- ❑ One black Sharpie
- ❑ One pack of thin markers
- ❑ One pack of twenty-four colored pencils
- ❑ One pencil box
- ❑ One roll of tape
- ❑ One pack of copy paper
- ❑ One box of facial tissue
- ❑ One large three-ring binder
- ❑ One pack of eight-tab subject dividers
- ❑ Two Glue Sticks
- ❑ One bottle of rubber cement
- ❑ Book covers
- ❑ Hand sanitizer
- ❑ Four folders with pockets (blue, yellow, red, and green)
- ❑ Lined index cards (3x5)
- ❑ One ruler displaying centimeters and inches
- ❑ One pack of construction paper
- ❑ One pack of graph paper

See a Book?
Check it out...

Name	Book	Date

How Do I Find
a Kind of Book?

Our Genres are color-coded:

Historical Fiction:

Science Fiction:

Realistic Fiction:

Non-Fiction:

Classics:

Daily Homework Log

Date	Subject	Assignment	Materials	Due Date
Monday				
Tuesday				
Wednesday				
Thursday				
Friday				

Weekly Cover Letter

Dear Parents,   Name _____

Attached is your child's work for the week of
_____. Please review the homework, class work, and
tests with your child and return the signed sheet on the following day.

You may keep the work at home.

If you have any questions or comments feel free to contact me, and I will address
any concerns as soon as possible.
Please make sure to return only the signed sheet.

Thank you for helping to make this a successful one. We appreciate your support.

Sincerely,

Signature_____ Date_____

Comments_____
_____
_____

Disciplinary Action

Student Name: _____

Teacher Name: _____

Date: _____

Time: _____

Behavior Infraction:

_____
_____
_____
_____
_____
_____
_____

Plan of Action:

      Silent lunch   Isolated Recess   Parent Contacted

Morning/Afternoon Detention (date/time)_____

Conference with parent (date/time)_____

Conference with counselor (date/time)_____

Conference with principal (date/time)_____

In-school suspension (date(s)/time)_____

Out-of-school suspension (date(s)/time)_____

Teacher Signature: _____

Student Signature: _____

Parent Signature: _____

Administration Signature: _____
(If applicable)

Homework Notice

Name:_____

Teacher: _____

Date:_____

Missing Work

Vocab: _____

Spelling:_____

English:_____

Science: _____

English:_____

History:_____

Social Studies:_____

Math: _____

Reading:_____

Completed at School   Yes   No

Due Tomorrow?   Yes   No

_____

Parent Signature

Notes:

Homework Notice

Name:_____

Teacher: _____

Date:_____

Missing Work

Vocab: _____

Spelling:_____

English:_____

Science: _____

English:_____

History:_____

Social Studies:_____

Math: _____

Reading:_____

Completed at School   Yes   No

Due Tomorrow?   Yes   No

_____

Parent Signature

Notes:

The Edutainer's Professional Agenda

Job or task to be completed	Person to complete the job (self/parent/ asst./student)	Necessary materials, directions, or arrangements	Date to be completed

Volunteers Needed

Volunteer Opportunity	Volunteer Parent(s)
Book Orders	
Volunteer(s) will prepare order forms, collect the monthly order, and distribute once the books arrive	1)
	2)
Phone Tree	1)
Three volunteers will call class parents when necessary	2)
	3)
Teacher Assistant Parents	1)
Assist by cutting out items, tracing, etc.	2)
	3)
Party Coordinator	1)
Volunteer will coordinate class parties	2)
	3)
Field Trip Coordinator	1)
Help coordinate field trips for the class	2)

Reading Parent Sign-up

When:

Reading Date	Reading Parent	Contact Number

Library Parent Sign-up

Note: Each parent will select ten books from the library related to holidays, the season, and unit of study or appropriate literature.

Month	Library Parent	Contact Number

Date _____

Dear Students,

I am so excited about being in fourth grade and having you as my class. For as long as I can remember I knew I'd be a teacher. The idea of helping students help themselves and really enjoy learning is very exciting! As for my past teaching, I have taught first, fourth, fifth, sixth, seventh, and eighth grade at public and private schools; I also believe I have learned just as much from my students as they have from me. Learning is meant to be shared and enjoyed. I plan to show you how to do both.

I am also a mother and a wife. Mr. McElroy and I have been married for a long time and have two sons. We also have a dog named O'Malley who is very much a part of our family. It's hard to believe the summer is actually behind us. My family and I spent a lot of time on the ball fields this summer. I love watching football, baseball, and I am just learning to understand lacrosse. We also enjoy the beach and snow skiing as a family, too. You just can't beat the long lazy days of June, July, and some of August, especially if you are at a pool. I really enjoy a great book and a comfortable chair near the water.

I am so excited about working with each and every one of you. My two goals for the year are to encourage you to love learning and take responsibility for your own success. Like every activity, you must choose to be an active player. Each of us enters the classroom with our own talents and gifts. I look forward to seeing yours grow. Let's make this a great year. Welcome to the fourth grade; you have arrived!

Sincerely,

Mrs. McElroy

OPEN HOUSE

Welcome to Fourth Grade
With Mrs. Lyskawa, Mrs. McElroy and Mrs. Readon
Tuesday, August 26, 2008

Curriculum:

*Reading: Houghton Mifflin text and novels (comprehensive/ clarification skills/ emphasis is on reading to learn rather than learning to read and applying literary terms to different genres)

*Cursive: Fourth grade students are required to use cursive with the exception of spelling

*Language Arts: English (grammar), spelling, vocabulary, and writing with the use of the folder system

*Math: Multi-digit addition, subtraction, multiplication, division, algebra, geometry, fractions, decimals, and percents

*Science: Four sciences (life, physical, space, and earth)

*Social Studies: Harcourt Horizons United States History

*Geography: Map skills, regional, and state studies

Classroom Behavioral Plan:

1. Beads to bucks to cashing in
--help… we need donations for our "bead store"

2. Agenda Marks:
1st offense: warning
2nd offense: silent lunch
3rd offense: parent contact
4th offense: detention (student arrival at 7:30 am)

Open House

Agenda:
- How we use it
- Why it's important
- Student's responsibility (our hands-off policy is geared toward getting them prepared for the following years to come)
- Parent's initials are required daily

Spelling and Vocabulary:
- Spelling and vocabulary are assigned at the beginning of every week
- Spelling is due on Wed. and Fri. with weekly test on Fri.
- Vocabulary is due on Tues. and Thurs. with a weekly quiz on Thurs. (quizzes will be replaced with a test every five lessons)

Binder and its sections:
- Our key to being organized

Make-up work:
- If absent for TWO or more days, request in a.m. for 3:00 pick-up.

Late assignments:
- Assignments must have signed yellow ticket
- 20 points off for the first day late
- 50 points off for the second day late
- 0 for the third day (please note that we count turning in assignments as part of the grade, not just the completion of the work)

Lunch:
- We eat lunch at 12:30–1:00
- Bring a healthy snack for 9:00
- We snack while working, so nothing messy please

Open House

Communication via the computer:
- Updated once a week
- Not to replace agenda
- Provides an overview of the week, lists upcoming events, and important dates

Friday Folder:
- Contains weekly work for you to review; please sign and return only the signed coversheet
- Workbook pages are not included in this folder as all books are kept intact

Contacting us:
- We're here for you
- E-mails work best
- Scheduled conferences: all parents are expected to meet two times per year (sign-up sheets will be placed in front office)
- Report cards go home after each quarter

Housekeeping:
- The student handbook is a wealth of knowledge
- Please ensure that students are on time to school
- All students must be picked up in front office before 2:45 for early pick-up
- Students are required to use "yes ma'am and no ma'am" on campus

Birthday Celebrations:
- Keep treats simple and supply enough only for your child's homeroom

Class Holiday Parties:
- Off-campus parties are not allowed

Room Mothers:
- Please sign up if you are willing to serve

Quarterly Progress Report

In the ___ grade, academic work/grades are communicated in a weekly manner. Each Friday a folder displaying the work that was collected that week is sent home with your child. This provides an OVERVIEW of averages as some work may be graded but kept in workbooks such as math, science, or vocabulary.

We are approximately halfway through our grading period and want to make you aware of your child's performance in any academic subject with an average of an 80 or below.

Student:_____

Subject:_____

Average:_____

Date:_____

Recommendation(s):

Parent Signature_____

Pre-Conference Form

Dear Parents,
As we get close to conference time, I would like you to take a moment to fill out this sheet before our meeting. This will ensure that we cover any concerns that you may have. Also, it will become part of the file I have on your child. Please return this form back to school with your child. I look forward to seeing you soon.

Thank you!

Student Name:_____

Parent's Name:_____

Date:_____

My child's attitude about school is:
_____
_____
_____

I see strengths in my child's progress in these
areas:_____
_____
_____

I have concerns about my child's progress in these
areas:_____
_____
_____

Topics I would like to
discuss:_____
_____
_____

Meeting

We are scheduled to meet at:

Date: _____

Time: _____

Location: _____

   Teacher: _____

Meeting

We are scheduled to meet at:

Date: _____

Time: _____

Location: _____

   Teacher: _____

Meeting

We are scheduled to meet at:

Date: _____

Time: _____

Location: _____

   Teacher: _____

Meeting

We are scheduled to meet at:

Date: _____

Time: _____

Location: _____

   Teacher: _____

Meeting

We are scheduled to meet at:

Date: _____

Time: _____

Location: _____

   Teacher: _____

Meeting

We are scheduled to meet at:

Date: _____

Time: _____

Location: _____

   Teacher: _____

Dear Parents,

It has been a while since some of you signed up for a conference. I have you down for this
time_____ on this date_____ to discuss
_____. If this appointment is no longer convenient, please let me
know, so I can reschedule it for another conference. I look forward to talking with you about
your child's progress and having time for any questions or concerns you may have.
Thank you!

Sincerely,

Dear Parents,

It has been a while since some of you signed up for a conference. I have you down for this
time_____ on this date_____ to discuss
_____. If this appointment is no longer convenient, please let me
know, so I can reschedule it for another conference. I look forward to talking with you about
your child's progress and having time for any questions or concerns you may have.
Thank you!

Sincerely,

Conference Documentation

Student Name_____ **Date** _____

Those present:
1.   4.
2.   5.
3.   6.

Student's Strengths:
_____
_____
_____
_____

Student's Weaknesses/Parental Concerns/ Questions:
_____
_____
_____
_____

Plan of Action:
_____
_____
_____

Parent/Teacher Conference Form

Student Name_____ **Date** _____

Those present:

1.   4.
2.   5.
3.   6.

Teacher(s) Concerns:

Family Concerns:

Plan Of Action:

1.

2.

3.

4.

Student Signature_____ **Parent**_____

Teacher_____ **Administrator**_____

Parent Conference Log

Student_____

Date_____

Parent(s) present _____

Other persons in attendance_____

Student's positive aspects:
Concerns:
Possible Solutions:

Conference Guide and Record

Date:_____ School:_____

Child's name:_____ Parent's name:_____

Teacher:_____ Subject/grade:_____

<u>Pre-Conference Notes:</u>

<u>Academic Progress:</u>

<u>Personal Growth in Habits and Attitudes:</u>

<u>Cooperative Action Agreed Upon in Conference:</u>

_____   _____

Teacher's Signature   Parent's Signature

Portfolio Suggestions for Elementary Students

- ❑ Kindergarten: two self-portraits (one in August and May)
- ❑ Math samples (minimum of one per quarter or semester)
- ❑ Writing samples (minimum of one per quarter or semester)
- ❑ Student selected work (that reflects his best work)
- ❑ Progress reports
- ❑ Parent/teacher conference notes
- ❑ Anecdotal notes
- ❑ Copy of report card
- ❑ Weekly reports of importance
- ❑ Copies of deficiencies
- ❑ Any standardized testing

Bibliography

Barbour, A. (2000). *Louder than words: Nonverbal communication.* Retrieved from www.minoritycareernet.com.

Barker, C. (2000). *Cultural studies: Theory and practice.* London: Sage.

Charles, C. M. (1981). *Building classroom discipline.* New York: Longman.

Coloroso, B. (1994). *Kids are worth it! Giving your child the gift of inner discipline.* New York: Avon Books.

Creswell, J. W. (1998). *Qualitative inquiry and research design: Choosing among five traditions.* Thousand Oaks, CA: Sage.

DeMarrais, K., & Lapan, S. (Eds.). (2004). *Foundations for research: Methods of inquiry in education and the social sciences.* Mahwah, NJ: Erlbaum.

Dewey, J. (1997). *How we think.* Mineola, NY: Dover.

Donaldson, G. (2001). *Cultivating leadership in schools: Connecting people, purpose, and practice.* Williston, VT: Teachers College Press.

Dykhuizen, G. (1973). *The life and mind of John Dewey* (J. A. Boydston, Ed.). Carbondale: Southern Illinois University Press.

Gabriel, J. G. (2005). *How to thrive as a teacher leader.* Alexandria, VA: Association for Supervision and Curriculum Development.

Glasser, W. (1998). *The quality school: Managing students without coercion.* New York: Harper Perennial.

Glasser, W. (1998). *The quality school teacher.* New York: Harper Perennial.

Hall, S. (Ed.). (1992). *Culture, media, language: Working papers in cultural studies, 1972–79.* London: Routledge.

Heller, D. (2004) *Teachers wanted: Attracting and retaining good teachers.* Alexandria, VA: Association for Supervision and Curriculum Development.

Jones, F. (2000). *Tools for teaching*. Santa Cruz, CA: Frederic Jones & Associates, Inc.

Klaus, P. (2007). *The hard truth about soft skills: Workplace lessons smart people wish they'd learned sooner*. New York: Harper Collins.

Marzano, R. J., Marzano, J. S., & Pickering, D. J. (2003). *Classroom management that works: Research-based strategies for every teacher*. Alexandria, VA: Association for Supervision and Curriculum Development.

McLeod, J., Fisher, J., & Hoover, G. (2003). *The key elements of classroom management: Managing time and space, student behavior, and instructional strategies*. Alexandria, VA: Association for Supervision and Curriculum Development.

McRobbie, A. (2005). *The uses of cultural studies*. London: Sage.

Nestle, M. (2002). *Food politics*. Los Angeles: University of California Press.

Neuman, S. (1985). Television and children's reading behavior. *Book Research Quarterly*, 83 (5), 63–67.

Noddings, N. (1998). *Philosophy of education*. Boulder, CO: Westview.

Reynolds, W. M. (2006). Cultural curriculum studies, multiplicity, and cinematic-machines. *Journal of Curriculum Theorizing* (22), 2.

Robinson, T., Borzekowski, D., Matheson, D., & Kraemer, H. (2007). Effects of fast food branding on young children's taste preferences. *Archives of Pediatrics & Adolescent Medicine*, 161, 792–797.

Sardar, Z. (2004). *Introducing cultural studies*. Thriplow, UK: Icon Books.

Schor, J. (1992). *The overworked American: The unexpected decline of leisure*. New York: Perseus Books. (See page 29.)

Simplicio, J. S. (1999). Some simple and yet overlooked common sense tips for a more effective classroom environment. *Journal of Instructional Psychology*, 26(2), 111.

Slack, J. D. (1996). The theory and method of articulation in cultural studies. In D. Morely & K. H. Chen (Eds.), *Stuart Hall: Critical dialogues in cultural studies* (112–127). London: Routledge.

Storey, J. (2001). *Cultural theory and popular culture*. New York: Prentice Hall.

Stronge, J. H. (2002). *Qualities of effective teachers*. Alexandria, VA: Association for Supervision and Curriculum Development.

Tauber, R. T. (1999). *Classroom management: Sound theory and effective practice* (third ed.). Westport, CT: Bergin & Garvey.

Williamson, B. (1993). *A first-year teacher's guidebook for success: A step-by-step educational recipe book from September to June*. Sacramento, CA: Dynamic Teaching Company.

Wilmore, E. (2007). *Teacher leadership: Improving teaching and learning from inside the classroom*. Thousand Oaks, CA: Corwin Press.

Wong, H., & Wong, R. (1998). *The first days of school*. Mountain View, CA: Harry K. Wong Publications, Inc.

Zehm, S. J., & Kottler, J. A. (1993). *On being a teacher: The human dimension*. Newbury Park, CA: Corwin Press.

About the Authors

Brad Johnson has over fourteen years of experience in the educational field. This includes experience in public schools, independent schools, and at the collegiate level. His degrees include a bachelor's degree in education, master's degree in education, specialist degree in leadership/administration, and a doctorate in curriculum studies from Georgia Southern University. He used cultural studies as his theoretical framework for his doctoral dissertation, *The Oppression of Obesity*. Dr. Johnson's educational certifications include science, educational leadership, instructional supervision, and teacher support specialist. Because of the diversity and extensive nature of his education background, Dr. Johnson has a unique perspective as it relates to education. His roles have included classroom teacher, administrator, curriculum developer, and scholarly researcher.

Besides his experiences as a teacher, curriculum director, and administrator, Dr. Johnson has served as an accreditation committee chair. He developed and supervised a formal mentoring program. He has chaired committees for curriculum development at the middle and high school levels. He has served on a board-level educational committee for an independent school. He has done quantitative studies on the effectiveness of educational initiatives such as brain-based learning and outdoor education. Dr. Johnson's research interest is in cultural studies, where his focus is on pop culture and its influence on students and learning.

Tammy Maxson McElroy has over twenty years of experience in the educational field. This experience includes teaching in public and independent schools. She has also edited books for publishing in different fields. Her degrees include a bachelor's degree in language arts and a master's degree in mathematics. Tammy's certifications include language arts, science, and mathematics. Her roles have included teacher, department chairperson, grade-level coordinator, and mentor, and she has served on committees that addressed the development of curriculum, textbook adoption, and admission test design, as well as schoolwide behavior and discipline policies.

During her time in public schools, Tammy served on a county-level committee to develop testing policies for one of the largest school systems in Georgia. She also served as department chairperson, where she mentored new teachers, developed a scope and sequence curriculum, and was involved in textbook adoption. During her tenure in independent schools, Tammy served on curriculum, leadership, and technological committees that developed policies as well as a scope and sequence curriculum for initial SACS certification for the school. She was instrumental in the development of the math and language arts curriculum for the middle and lower school. Tammy was instrumental in the implementation of a formal mentoring program for new teachers.

*For more information on the authors, please visit www.EncoreEdutainment.com.